Global Credit Management

Wiley Finance Series

Global Credit Management

An Executive Summary

Ron Wells
CCE ACMA FCIS ACIB

John Wiley & Sons, Ltd

Other Wiley Editorial Offices

John Wiley & Sons Inc., 111 River Street, Hoboken, NJ 07030, USA

Jossey-Bass, 989 Market Street, San Francisco, CA 94103-1741, USA

Wiley-VCH Verlag GmbH, Boschstr. 12, D-69469 Weinheim, Germany

John Wiley & Sons Australia Ltd, 33 Park Road, Milton, Queensland 4064, Australia

John Wiley & Sons (Asia) Pte Ltd, 2 Clementi Loop #02-01, Jin Xing Distripark, Singapore 129809

John Wiley & Sons Canada Ltd, 22 Worcester Road, Etobicoke, Ontario, Canada M9W 1L1

Wiley also publishes its books in a variety of electronic formats. Some content that appears in print may not
be available in electronic books.

Library of Congress Cataloging-in-Publication Data

Wells, Ron.
    Global credit management : an executive summary / Ron Wells.
        p. cm.
    Includes bibliographical references and index.
    ISBN 0-470-85111-2 (cloth)
    1. International business enterprises—Finance.   2. Credit departments—Management.
    3. Credit—Management.   4. Risk management.
    I. Title.
    HG4027.5.W45 2003
    658.8'8—dc22   2003019196

British Library Cataloguing in Publication Data

A catalogue record for this book is available from the British Library

ISBN 0-470-85111-2

Typeset in 10/12pt Times by Originator, Gt Yarmouth, Norfolk
Printed and bound in Great Britain by Antony Rowe Ltd, Chippenham, Wiltshire
This book is printed on acid-free paper responsibly manufactured from sustainable forestry
in which at least two trees are planted for each one used for paper production.

Contents

Preface

Credit has the power to drive your business beyond your ambition. Effectively harness this power and it will prove the foundation of your success. Let this power out of your control and it could destroy all your efforts to build a flourishing enterprise.

Harnessing credit power is the responsibility of every employee, just as it is the responsibility of every executive. Avoiding the negative propensities of credit power is an equal responsibility.

Loss of creditworthiness, loss of trust, can drive a healthy business to ruin, just as a substantial amount of bad debt can bankrupt a company.

Credit power propels modern commerce and industry. In yesteryear credit power enabled Henry Ford to make mass production work. If his customers had been forced to "save up" to buy the Model-T, the demand-pull to justify mass production would not have existed. Henry's great achievement would not have seen the light of day.

Today the emphasis is on supply chains, rather than mass production, but the fact is that credit power is the grease that keeps these virtual production lines functioning.

Credit is about trust and trust is like truth, just as truth is like reality. As reality changes so what is true one day may not be true the next. Hence as circumstances change, what can be trusted today may not be trusted tomorrow. Thus harnessing credit power is about understanding that credit is believing a future event (being paid on time) will occur. Not on the grounds of faith. On the grounds of understanding the forces that will cause that event to occur.

Take credit power by the throat, understand the forces that drive people to pay or not to pay. Understand how to make those forces press home their influence at the right moment.

Likewise, take control of the credit profile of your business and see your fortunes blossom. Suppliers will rush to fill your purchase orders, and bankers will inundate you with offers of money.

Establish confidence you will pay and be paid. Then you will be able to expand your business aggressively, yet safely. You will power past your competitors and survive "the slings and arrows of outrageous fortune" (*Hamlet*, III. i. 58).

Discover the vital life force of your business through the medium of this book, discover *credit power*.

Ron Wells

Part I
Credit Power and Business Development: The Strategic Overview

1

Why Grant Credit?

1.1 INTRODUCTION

Many executives conclude that *a certain level of receivable balances outstanding permanently is an inevitable cost of doing business* and assign the task of credit management a status equivalent to that of routine housekeeping, like clearing waste-bins or deciding which brand of toilet paper to purchase.

Deciding who to grant credit, when and how much. Allowing transactions to go ahead "on credit" and following up to collect the money. In many quarters the perception is that these are not glamorous tasks, they add only costs, they are chores undertaken perforce, not by choice, like vacuuming the house, or sweeping up fallen leaves.

Old Style Executive (OSEx): (Thinks) I am in business therefore I give credit. (Says to Human Resources person) You better hire some pesky "business prevention officers", but be sure to employ less than we need and pay them "peanuts". Can't afford any more non-contributors draining away my quarterly bonus, but must keep those investment analysts off my back.

HR person: Okay, Boss.

This attitude is good news for executives who hold the opposing view. It hands them a competitive advantage on a silver platter!

Granting credit to customers – buyers of your goods and/or services – is not simply a natural outcome of being in business. "I am in business therefore I give credit" is *not* a natural law.

Credit is a powerful strategic tool in the hands of a competitive entrepreneur. It should be fashioned and moulded, given or withheld, in accordance with the strategic interest of the business.

New Style Executive (NSEx): Great news! OSEx has just told his professional credit manager to stop wasting time on ideas and focus on traditional methods of micro-managing accounts!

On average, businesses have about 28% of their assets invested in outstanding receivable account balances. These balances form a large part of working capital, and freeze cash out of reach. As an (admittedly extreme) example, BP had more than US$26 billion locked up in receivables as at 31 December 2001.

In the twenty-first century – the information age – a growing proportion of enterprises (such as trading, hospitality, information and knowledge-based businesses) have a relatively small fixed asset base, leading to an even heavier weighting of receivable balances on their balance sheets.

In addition to the impact on a company's balance sheet structure, receivable balances impact liquidity and cost of capital. Therefore a decision to grant credit is an important investment decision, with strategic implications. Armed with this understanding, it is easy to conclude that giving credit is a decision not to be taken lightly:

NSEx: Hire the best receivables portfolio strategist available. Offer a seat on the Executive Committee. I don't want cash frozen without purpose, our cash has to work for us 24/365!

People Manager: I know just the person. Thought you'd want the best.

No business "has to give credit". The innate power of credit either to propel a business forward, or to bring it to its knees, requires that every business should consciously decide whether to grant credit and, if yes, on what terms. In every case these strategic decisions should be made at the highest level and reviewed regularly.

When executives consider credit strategy questions they take into account the reasons why it may be prudent to offer credit, the tactics available to be employed in managing that credit day to day, and the ways in which the often significant balance sheet impact of credit decisions can be optimized. These considerations give rise to a formal credit policy to guide the day-to-day micromanagement of individual buyer accounts.

Strategic reasons for granting credit fall in five main categories, as detailed below.

1.2   PRODUCT OFFER ENHANCEMENT CREDIT STRATEGY

The basis of this strategy is the belief that a customer faced with a choice between a certain product "without credit" or "with credit" would choose to buy from the seller offering credit. Supplier credit is, generally speaking, the cheapest form of short-term finance, hence its importance as a part of the mix of features of any product offer. Thus if a company's product is already competitive on grounds of price, quality and delivery, it may be enhanced by adding credit terms:

NSEx: Why are we offering credit terms with this product? We're not a bank!

Sales Executive (SEx): Well all our competitors offer credit.

NSEx: Unacceptable answer! Our product is superior. Buyers are climbing over each other to buy from us, we should let their bankers do the financing.

SEx: Well no, Boss, our competitors match us on quality, price and delivery. If we withdraw credit we'll have to offer something to compensate or we'll lose business!

Alternatively a business may decide to add credit terms as a feature in order to equal its competitors, or to enhance its credit terms in order to better the competition.

The impact of this strategy will usually be that those companies that have better quality credit analysis, and/or are less risk averse, and/or employ the best tactics to minimize credit risk, and/or have the largest margin available to absorb credit losses (through receivables not collected and/or late payment) will be the most successful competitors in the medium to long term. This emphasizes the need for good quality, yet aggressive, commercially minded credit management.

1.3   COMPARATIVE COST OF MONEY CREDIT STRATEGY

If it is cheaper for a supplier to borrow money than it is for its buyer, a potential "win–win" situation arises that can additionally provide a competitive advantage. A supplier could provide credit but simultaneously increase its margin to recoup the additional cost of capital incurred. If the cost of money difference is sufficient between the seller's jurisdiction and the buyer's, the overall cost of the goods should nevertheless be lower than it would be if the buyer used local finance, hence the description "win–win".

SEx: (To Credit Executive) Our distributor in Ukraine can't afford to increase purchases to meet local demand. He simply can't afford to borrow funds at 40% p.a. to pay cash in advance.

Credit Executive (CEx): We can borrow funds at 4% p.a. If I can cover the payment and transfer risks for less than 6% p.a., could we do a deal? We'll have to recover our extra costs!

SEx: Sure! He could eat 10% p.a. and still make a tidy profit. It's another "win–win" for proactive credit!

Any supplier utilizing this strategy must, however, take into account any negative effect buyer receivable risk may have on its cost of capital. Cost of capital will be discussed in more detail in another chapter. Suffice it to record at this point that the greater the risk inherent in a company's receivable portfolio, the greater the cost of borrowing funds or raising capital to fund its activities. Hence it is vital that all ramifications of granting credit are carefully weighed when calculating the net present value of such a decision, compared to the net present value of a decision not to grant credit:

CEx: Have you weighed all the ramifications?

SEx: Of course! They're all included in the margin!

CEx: Hmmmm. (Thinks) I hear a band playing "Believe that if you like!"

1.4   CREDIT STRATEGY FOR ADMINISTRATIVE EFFICIENCY

The granting of trade credit may be motivated by a desire to capture certain administrative efficiencies and thus reduce operating costs. Efficiencies available include: reducing numbers of invoices, reducing cash handling, reducing numbers of shipments, reducing storage costs, and increasing sales volumes (i.e. reducing fixed costs per item).

Cash in advance (CIA) or cash on delivery (COD) payment terms require the issue of an invoice with each order and, in the latter case, the handling of cash by delivery personnel. Where CIA terms are used in relation to the almost continuous delivery of goods – such as the provision of jet fuel to airlines – quantities and prices have to be estimated prior to delivery, resulting in extensive reconciliation work and the risk of unauthorized credit exposures arising from time to time. The related administrative costs, unplanned credit risks and security risks can be avoided, and deliveries can be speeded up, if formal credit terms are granted.

It may be necessary in many circumstances for suppliers to introduce minimum order quantity restrictions, to avoid incurring excessive freight and handling costs. In these instances buyers unable to pay in advance for such a large order will require assistance through the provision of supplier credit.

On the other hand, in cases where the cost of storage of seasonal goods is lower at the point of consumption or sale than at the place of production, it is advantageous for producers to shift this burden to their buyers. Trade credit often plays a key role in enabling relevant markets to capture this efficiency.

The prime example of this credit strategy is provided by the agricultural fertilizer market. Manufacturers of chemical fertilizer operate a year-round production cycle but farmers only utilize fertilizer during a short period prior to planting. Farmers usually have cheaper storage facilities for fertilizer than those that could be provided for such quantities at the places of production. There are also transport savings available if fertilizer is shipped steadily throughout the year, rather than in a concentrated pre-season period. However, the only way to capture the potential storage and transport savings for the fertilizer and agricultural industries is for the manufacturers to grant supplier credit to farmers, from the time of delivery until the farmers realize cash from the sale of related crops.

Supplier credit can increase sales volumes thus enabling manufacturers to capture economies of scale and to reduce the proportion of fixed overheads per item produced. A good example of this is car manufacturers offering 0% financing incentive programmes, to encourage buyers to bring forward their purchase decisions and thus increase near-term sales volumes.

Furniture Bob: Sign this magic finance agreement and you can take your chairs away today! Why wait to accumulate cash? Pay nothing for a year and a day! Sign up right away!

Furniture Buyer: Do you have a pen I could use?

1.5   CREDIT STRATEGY TO BUILD TRUST

The granting of credit can powerfully signal (a) that the supplier has confidence in the quality of the goods or services supplied and/or (b) that the supplier wants to establish a long-term relationship with the buyer.

A seller may overcome any reluctance to buy its product by effectively allowing the purchaser time to check the goods before payment becomes due. This signals confidence in the value provided by the product, and confidence that the purchaser will want to buy more in future.

Seller: We are so confident you'll like these z4x widgets and be desperate to have more, we offer open credit terms on your first purchase.

Buyer: Okay, I'll take two dozen!

It has been traditional to begin a new relationship with a buyer on "cash in advance" or "letter of credit" terms. As the relationship then develops over several years, terms would progress through "promissory note" and "documentary collections" until the relationship eventually matured to reach the state of "open credit". Thus open credit terms have come to be associated with long-term relationships founded on mutual knowledge, respect and trust. It may no longer be possible to develop commercial relationships so gradually, but open credit terms are still powerfully connected with mutual trust and the desire for a long-term association. Good quality credit management, based on good quality information and/or credit risk mitigation techniques, can enable open credit terms as a compelling indicator of trust – a key marketing device – even in cases where the relationship has not matured.

Seller: Your payment terms will be "open credit".

Buyer: Thank you, that will be very helpful. (Thinks) They trust and respect me. They obviously want a long-term relationship, yippee! I must phone their competitor tomorrow and cancel our meeting.

1.6   CREDIT STRATEGY FOR BUSINESS DEVELOPMENT

In some situations potential distributors may be start-up businesses without significant working capital and/or may be operating in a jurisdiction where it is not possible to raise venture capital or short-term bank finance. If a supplier is not prepared to create its own local branch or subsidiary to distribute and promote the sale of its products, it could assist its distributor by providing working capital through extended supplier credit. This would entail allowing the distributor to delay payment until it had actually received cash from end-user buyers or consumers. Terms such as "180 days after shipment date" or "60 days after the goods leave the distributor's warehouse" could be negotiated, depending on local conditions.

CEx: (To Kazakh distributor) How many days from invoice date do you need?

Kazakh distributor (KD): Sixty or maybe 90.

CEx: Well let's work this out. Twenty days transport and customs clearance, plus 5 days to move the goods to your depots. You're selling 20 cartons a day, on average, so add 35 days in inventory, and how long does it take to collect cash from your buyers?

KD: About 25 days.

CEx: Okay, say another 30 days, that's 90 days in total.

KD: Yes, as I said!

An arrangement such as this would increase administrative and monitoring costs, and increase the risk of loss due to bad debts, but the negatives should be weighed against the long-term benefits of developing a successful local distributor. Nonetheless any potential loss should not be excessive because "there's no long-term if you can't survive the short-term" (Lawton, 2002).

1.7 CONCLUSION

The case for proactive decision making regarding credit strategy at the highest level of any organization is clear. Credit is potentially a powerful tool available to executives crafting an effective marketing strategy. If its potential is understood and used wisely, credit will promote success in the most competitive of circumstances. Conversely, those business leaders who accept credit passively, as a necessary chore, and leave it to meander through the enterprise without strategic direction, will ensure that credit adds little and will risk a credit-related disaster arising without warning:

Credit Analyst 2 (CAn2): (New in the organization) If only we had some strategic direction we'd know where to concentrate our resources.

Credit Analyst 1 (CAn1): (Been in place for a while) Don't worry, our fearless leader OSEx has everything under control. You just focus on catching up last year's annual account reviews. OSEx will take care of today and tomorrow.

CAn2: I just don't like nasty surprises . . . I lost my last job 'cause no one saw the broken rail ahead of the Enron locomotive.

2

Customer Risk

2.1 IT'S PEOPLE! PEOPLE MAKE THE DIFFERENCE!

Chief Financial Officer (CFO): Stop, stop, stop! Please don't mention another ratio! Ratios don't run businesses, and ratios won't save your job, Stanley! Tell me about the people in the company! Who's in charge? What did you see when you asked straight questions face to face? We've a lot of money riding on this distributor!

Stanley: But, Boss, their balance sheet is strong, they're making profits, and the trade references check out. I thought a visit would be a waste of time.

CFO: What? You haven't met these people! You haven't seen the premises, met the staff! Stanley, we've hundreds of thousands already invested, and they're sucking in more cash every day! Obviously their cash cycle needs review and close attention, but you don't even know if they have a real business!

Stanley: Their accounts are audited . . .

CFO: Don't interrupt! You sit in your comfortable office and process paper records. What are you? A failed archaeologist? Couldn't take the fieldwork so you fell into credit management by accident? Go out of my office, go out of the building, take a plane, take a train, walk if necessary, find out what's happening with this distributor. Find out about the people, are they manipulating the ratios to keep you off their backs? Or are the ratios truly a result of the real business they're developing? Do they have a sustainable competitive advantage? Between the time they collect and the time they eventually pay, what are they doing with our money? Do they have a sideline? Do they all drive top of the range BMWs or modest VWs? Do some fieldwork, do some digging, who are their customers? How do they control their receivables? Do they know what time of day it is?

Stanley: Boss, I just came back from vacation, my work's backed up, I can't . . .

CFO: You're not listening, Stanley. Don't wait 'til they're bankrupt to find time for creditors' committee meetings, visit tomorrow! You know how to run a business. You know how to describe and analyse the cash cycle. You can advise them how to organize to generate cash to pay us on time. Do it! Don't spend your time with useless ratios that tell me about one day three months ago! Wake up, Stanley, the power of credit is not unlocked through ratio analysis!

Stanley: But our audit report suggested annual reviews with ratio analysis . . .

CFO: The future is where we will be paid or not paid! Cash is what we will be paid with. You won't find any future in balance sheet ratio analysis! You won't find a cash flow forecast in ratio analysis! You won't find out about market risk through ratio analysis!

You won't find out about management honesty through ratio analysis! You won't find much future in your job if you don't meet these people and give me a full report next week!

2.2   DUE DILIGENCE

The first priority in the case of any customer (foreign or domestic) must be to establish whether it operates a genuine business. Your credit team must establish the full and correct name of every buyer, its registered and main trading address(es), and the names of the owners or active executives. This information will be invaluable should you ever need to try to collect money due to your company. Obtain a credit agency report to confirm basic details about each customer, such as the legal status of the business and other publicly available data.

The best form of due diligence is a personal visit to the prospective buyer. Some useful questions to answer during such a visit are:

- Are the staff busy and do they seem efficient in going about their business?
- Does the new customer market any other familiar brand names that could provide references?
- Is there evidence of extravagant living?

A personal visit is also an opportunity to start building a relationship of mutual respect that will pay dividends when problems and misunderstandings arise.

If your budget does not allow a visit specifically for this purpose, a questionnaire should be designed for your Sales Manager to complete, after meeting with a customer. In addition, corroborating information should be obtained by using diplomatic or consular missions, banks, credit agencies, the CIA website, chambers of commerce and the Internet generally.

In the event that no one from your company has met a customer you should be very wary indeed. The business you are asked to deliver goods or services to may be a sham, it may not exist at all.

2.2.1   Credit fraud

Credit frauds are usually based on a careful study of the traditional methods used in reaching credit decisions. Armed with this knowledge the criminal sets about manipulating the credit process in order to obtain goods without payment.

There are three types of scheme: (a) the "shell company" fraud, (b) the "bust-out" fraud and (c) the theft of corporate identity. A "shell company" fraud involves setting up a company and investing it with a completely false legitimacy. Incorporation information, a telephone listing, trade references that seem genuine, a website, and even a credit report based solely on data submitted by the criminal. All of this is designed to dupe a supplier or suppliers into delivering goods on open credit terms. The "business" closes and the criminals disappear when they have completed the deception.

A "bust-out" requires the fraudsters to invest capital and is the most complex ploy. A company with a good credit record is either acquired, or fabricated through genuine trading. The criminals then embark on a buying spree and the goods are sold, without the intention of paying the suppliers.

A theft of corporate identity is usually a simple scam involving a criminal pretending to represent a legitimate company, that has a good credit record, when ordering goods.

The perpetrators of credit fraud are fairly predictable, so an active programme of preventative measures is usually effective. The first step is to understand the extent of the threat and the weaknesses in your company systems. Procedures can then be implemented to eliminate any opportunities available to the criminal fraternity.

2.3   CUSTOMER PAYMENT RISK

Customer risk is defined as the risk that a buyer will fail to pay, either due to *financial constraints* (bankruptcy or illiquidity) or due to *dishonesty* (indefinite payment delays without good reason).

Liquidity and honesty are distinct from other possible reasons for failure to pay, in that they are under the direct and active control of the management of the buyer. A successful seller/buyer relationship requires that the buyer's management must be honest, must be capable of effectively operating its business day to day, and must be capable of dealing with any crisis that may arise. Hence a perceptive assessment of the ability of the management of a customer (buyer) is as important as a competent assessment of the financial and commercial information available for analysis.

High-quality trade credit analysis can provide a competitive advantage while protecting your company from suffering catastrophic losses, due to cash flow interruptions (late payments) or buyer bankruptcy (actual loss of revenue). Analysis aims to determine whether a customer "can pay" and "will pay"; bearing in mind that "credit is an option to default".

The well-known, serious limitations of traditional credit analysis methods were sharply brought into focus by the Enron event. That, and other similar shocks, led *Business Week* (2002) to remark: "Excessive Pay, Weak Leadership, Corrupt Analysts, Complacent Boards, Questionable Accounting, Enough Already!"

A study by von Stein and Ziegler (1984, quoted in Altman and Narayanan, 1997) attempted to identify the characteristics and concrete behavioural indications that distinguish failed firms from solvent ones. The qualities found to set failed company management apart (from those in the non-failed group) were the following:

- Being out of touch with reality
- Large technical knowledge but poor commercial control
- Great talents in salesmanship
- Strong-willed
- Sumptuous living and unreasonable withdrawals (of cash from the business)
- Excessive risk-taking

The management of solvent companies was found to be more homogeneous than (that of) failed companies and seldom showed a lack of consciousness of reality. The authors recommend all three components of analysis (balance sheet, account behaviour and management) be pursued to assess a company.

Knight (1979, quoted in Altman and Narayanan, 1997) analysed the records of a large number of small business failures as well as conducting interviews with key persons involved. Knight [found that] some type of managerial incompetence accounts for almost all failures.

Traditional analysis does not generally uncover these key traits successfully. The result is a lot of reliance being placed on subjective evaluations fashioned by individual analysts. Although many argue that analysts generally reach an intuitive conclusion after weighing all the evidence, it is clear that traditional credit analysis is principally reliant on (a) financial ratio analysis and annual report-based reviews, (b) debt ratings provided by the big three agencies,[1] and (c) mathematical models that are based on questionable assumptions and that extrapolate the past.

Yet it is evident that incompetent or dishonest management can lead a company with a "strong" balance sheet and a great track record to failure, whereas a competent and honest management can turn around a failing company with a "weak" balance sheet and poor track record. People make the difference, which is why – scientific though it may be – financial analysis provides only a starting point for credit analysis, it does not identify those companies that will fail, until after the event.

Powerful credit analysis must focus on identifying companies that will fail, well before they declare bankruptcy, and those that will fail to pay your company even though they have the money to meet their obligations. The traditional approach to customer credit analysis has to be reinvented, starting from the assertion that "a lot of empirical evidence exists to suggest companies most often fail due either to *management dishonesty* or *management incompetence*".

When you set out to reinvent customer credit analysis as a powerful value-creating instrument within your company, you have a range of ingredients with which to work, detailed as follows.

2.4 CUSTOMER RISK ANALYSIS TOOLS

The most important tools available to support a credit analysis process are:

- Financial information as to the condition and achievements of the customer or potential customer. This is usually in the form of a balance sheet, an income statement (or profit and loss account), a cash flow statement, an auditor's report, and explanatory notes.
- Information relating to the future plans and strategies of the customer. This may be available through executive announcements or media releases, and cash flow forecasts. Such either accompany the publication of financial results or are published ad hoc.
- Payment and operational performance information gleaned from other suppliers (credit references), banks (bank references), your company's own records, credit reference agencies (credit information suppliers), the Internet, and public records, such as court files and newspapers.

---

[1] The big three credit rating agencies are: *Fitch IBCA* (http://www.fitchibca.com), Moody's Investor Services (http://www.moodys.com) and *Standard & Poor's* (http://www.sandp.com).

- Generally available information regarding the customer's industry and market environment, together with information regarding the legal and tax environment in which the customer operates.
- Personal visits to the customer's premises and market.

2.5   ANALYSIS OF FINANCIAL INFORMATION

Financial information supplied by your customer, even if it is accompanied by a "clean" auditor's report, must be considered with extreme care. The first point to bear in mind is that any such information is a record of the past, which does not necessarily indicate what the buyer's position is in the present or will be in the future.

The *balance sheet* is particularly "static" and particularly vulnerable to manipulation. It is "static" in that it represents the asset, liability and equity position at the close of business on a particular day. The picture before and after that instant in time will be different. In terms of generally accepted accounting practices a great deal of flexibility is allowed management and auditors in determining how various transactions, assets and liabilities should be represented in financial statements. Hence it is vital to read and critically analyse all the notes that accompany financial statements.

Income statements suffer from the drawback of being vulnerable to manipulation through the flexibility allowed by generally accepted accounting practices. In particular the use of the accrual method (which entails profit and loss adjustments not related to cash flow) can give a distorted picture of the buyer's achievements. This can lead to cash being paid out to shareholders (in the form of dividends) and to tax authorities at a time of cash shortage.

Most credit analysts utilize well-known *financial-statement-based ratios* to determine their credit decisions. This approach is fully understood throughout commerce and industry, so unscrupulous executives are able to manipulate credit analysts' decisions. They simply manipulate balance sheet and income statement figures to produce "desired" ratios.

Customer risk relates specifically (a) to the availability of cash to meet payable commitments on due date and (b) to the willingness of the customer's management to pay.

The *cash flow statement* is the most reliable of those documents that usually form a customer's set of financial statements. It reflects actual cash movements during the review period so it will provide the information needed to understand:

- The customer's *ability to generate cash*
- The customer's strategy for the *utilization of cash* generated
- *Sources of cash* utilized during the year
- The *cash flow cycle* of the customer's business, and
- The customer's "*defensive interval*"

A customer's "defensive interval" is the time (expressed in days) during which the customer can continue to operate its business utilizing only cash resources (liquid assets) actually on hand on the relevant balance sheet date.

Defensive Interval = Quick Assets/Daily Cash Operating Expenses

The number calculated for the "defensive interval" indicates how many days the "defensive assets" can continue to support normal operations despite a complete cessation of revenues. The "revenue cessation" concept provides a base measure from which one can assess the financial reserves available to the company. It makes possible the direct comparison of a company with its competitor or peer companies.

The "cash flow cycle" is the time required to convert goods into cash; from the date the company pays the costs of acquisition of the goods to the date of receipt of the cash from related sales:

$$\text{Cash Flow Cycle} = (\text{Days Inventory} + \text{Days Sales Outstanding}) - \text{Days Payables}$$

$$\text{Days Inventory} = \text{Inventory}/(\text{Cost of Sales}/365)$$

$$\text{Days Sales Outstanding} = \text{Trade Receivables}/(\text{Sales}/365)$$

$$\text{Days Payables} = \text{Trade Accounts Payable}/(\text{Cost of Sales}/365)$$

The cash flow cycle clearly indicates why situations that feature increasing sales and/or increasing prices create a significant demand for cash. Cash is locked up in the cash flow cycle of every business. Action to effectively reduce the cash flow cycle will automatically unlock cash.[2]

2.5.1   However reported, operating cash flow can be misleading...

The operating cash flow section of the cash flow statement is the most useful indicator available as to the enduring cash generation ability of a business. It is also a useful reference point for an analyst seeking to identify balance sheet and income statement manipulations:

> Unfortunately, cash flow, especially operating cash flow, is not immune to the creative practices of the financial numbers game. Moreover, even in the absence of attempts by some managements to mislead, unexpected vagaries in the manner in which operating cash flow is defined can be misleading. (Mulford and Comiskey, 2002: 354)

Generally accepted accounting practices mean the following aspects require particular attention, investigation and careful analysis. In many cases reported operating cash flow figures will have to be adjusted as a result of such analysis. The objective is to reflect more accurately the level of cash flow that a company can be expected to sustain from continuing operations.

- Income generated by businesses discontinued (sold or closed) during a fiscal year is usually included in reported operating cash flow. The inclusion of this number in operating cash flow is misleading since the business line that generated such income will, by definition, no longer contribute cash flow to future operations.
- All income taxes paid (after taking into account any tax credits or after-tax gains) are included in operating cash flow. This means that taxes paid and tax credits received that relate to investing or financing activities could distort the operating cash flow figures if significant. Since such taxes and after-tax gains relate to non-

---

[2] Refer to various publications and presentations by George Gallinger (Associate Professor of Finance, Arizona State University, Tempe) for more information about "cash flow analysis", the "cash flow cycle" and the "defensive interval" at http://www.public.asu.edu/~bac524/.

recurring activities – such as the sale of an investment or employee stock option tax benefits – they should be removed from operating cash flow.

- Cash flow generated as a result of securities trading activities that are sporadic (as opposed to being a continuous part of the business) will distort the operating cash flow figure unless an adjustment is effected.
- Expenditure that is treated as an asset on a company's balance sheet (capitalized expenditure) is another potential source of operating cash flow distortion. The acquisition of assets is classified as an "investing activity", hence the related negative cash flow does not impact the operating section of a cash flow statement. Furthermore any related amortization (depreciation) of the asset value, over its estimated economic life, is likewise considered a non-cash item and added to income, when operating cash flow is deduced in subsequent years. In cases where the assets purchased are not tangible and tend to be augmented by additional purchases year after year (such as software in the case of technology-intensive enterprises), failure to include the cash flow implications within the reported operating cash flow numbers, by treating the activity as an investment, will be misleading.

Armed with an awareness of the factors that can distort a cash flow statement (particularly the operating cash flow section) an analyst will usually find within the financial statements the information necessary to make appropriate adjustments.

2.6   ANALYSIS OF INFORMATION ABOUT THE FUTURE

Given the rapid pace of change being experienced *the future is less and less likely to resemble the past*. The challenge is to predict the probability that your customer's management will be able to successfully cope with the future. In order to make this evaluation a credit analyst needs to:

- Assess the customer's business environment and its competitors' possible strategies
- Understand the customer's resources and strategies, and
- Reach a reasoned decision as to the probable efficacy or otherwise of the customer's plans

The past (the customer's "track record"), and evidence of available resources and constraints (financial analysis), will be important starting points for the credit analyst. They may provide reliable *clues as to the customer's abilities to deal with the future*.

An assessment of a customer's future prospects must be continuously updated, as circumstances evolve. Someone in your organization must be charged with the duty to monitor all relevant news media reports, economic forecasts, rating agency updates, investment analyst pronouncements, legislative changes, tax changes, corporate press releases, and any other external sources. Monitoring should include internally generated information, such as payment performance, operational performance, and pertinent information gathered by all other parts of your business. The sales department is, for example, a valuable source of up-to-date intelligence. All information should be treated with the necessary degree of caution and scepticism, verified when possible, and used to adjust the credit opinion and credit terms of affected customers, when appropriate.

2.7 CREDIT SCORING

Important limitations are imposed on credit scoring when it is used in the corporate environment, as opposed to the retail or consumer environment:

- The number of customers with sufficiently similar characteristics to be grouped together for analytical purposes is usually *too small to provide statistically reliable indicators.*
- *Customers are able to manipulate the financial data* that is used as the foundation of most credit scoring models.
- The *past is not a reliable indicator of the future* in the corporate environment.
- All models contain several significant elements that *are based on the subjective decisions and assumptions* of the human model builders.
- Models *do not "transfer" successfully from one country to another.*

2.8 TRADE CREDIT RISK SCORECARD

A useful adaptation of the credit scoring approach is the development of Trade Credit ScoreCards. This technique uses the Balanced ScoreCard concept to create scoring models that require analysts to give due weight to non-financial factors when assessing credit risk. ScoreCards provide a logical and standardized framework for analysts to use when working through the examination of a customer's position, before making a credit decision.

The objectives of developing a ScoreCard are to:

- Make credit limit decisions in a standardized and systematic way, based on facts
- Make credit decisions that align with and support your company strategy
- Speed up credit decisions and enable the use of technology to a greater extent

In addition ScoreCard-based credit decisions can be enhanced to provide credit risk scores. Such risk scores need not be based on complex mathematics, nor on probability or "gaming" theory. They need not be processed through a "black box" neural network with weighting adjusted within the program. They can be based on simple weighting, with some easy-to-understand algebraic adjustments. They should be designed to ensure discrimination between various grades of risk in a transparent fashion.

The core intent of a ScoreCard is to *imitate* the thought processes of a team of highly experienced and qualified credit analysts, and thereby – on each occasion the ScoreCard is used – to reach the same conclusion that such a group of experts would have reached, using traditional methods.

Credit risk scores are useful in terms of receivable portfolio analysis and in ensuring that your company is adequately compensated for the risk carried when advancing trade credit. In order to develop a useful ScoreCard the designer has to take into account the requirements and peculiarities of your company, as well as those of your potential market. The model should be tested as extensively as possible before it is utilized. Subjective elements must be reviewed regularly. Refer to Chapter 14 to find a practical example of a Trade Credit Risk ScoreCard.

2.9   CUSTOMER LIMITS

When a decision is made to grant unsecured trade credit the next step is to decide how much exposure to allow, in other words where to set the credit limit. Three interdependent criteria should be considered when deciding the quantum of a limit.

Each unsecured limit should not exceed the maximum amount your company can bear to lose, through the failure of an individual customer. A useful guideline to this amount may be a proportion of your company's equity, say 10%. In other words, no matter how creditworthy or financially strong a customer appears to be, you should not be in a position where your company would lose more than one-tenth of its equity if that one customer failed to pay. This condition will impose a maximum cap on all individual limits.

Each limit amount should not exceed the customer's assessed ability to pay in the normal course of business. In this respect attention should be given to factors such as:

- The normal pattern of a customer's business
- Normal purchase levels
- Internal sales levels
- Usual credit terms prevalent in the customer's market
- The relative size of the customer's business, and
- Its relative financial strength

A limit amount should be sufficient to accommodate your customer's normal purchasing pattern. If it is not possible to meet this requirement, your company should explore the possibility of sharing the payment risk with a bank or credit insurance entity, transaction by transaction.

2.10   AUTHORITY TO APPROVE CREDIT LIMITS

The receivable portfolio of a company often represents a substantial entrepreneurial investment in the businesses of its customers, and often represents significant risk. Hence it is imperative that (a) carefully designed processes are in place, and (b) people with adequate experience and training are employed to manage such processes day to day. However, it is equally important that unified and firm control be exercised in respect of the granting of credit limits to customers, from the very top of your company.

All concerned should clearly understand that only designated employees are authorized to grant credit limits, in accordance with given policies and procedures. Furthermore that credit limits are set to limit credit exposure and, unless amended for good reason, credit limits have to be respected. All orders and subsequent exposures should be monitored regularly to ensure that limits are not exceeded. Immediate action should be taken to correct any identified transgression, either by obtaining third-party (bank or insurance company) security, obtaining early payment, preventing delivery of orders in process and future orders, or increasing the limit if justified.

The delegation of authority to grant unsecured credit limits (DoA) should be approved by your Board of Directors. It should delegate authority to the Chief Executive Officer (CEO), allowing further delegation to the Chief Financial Officer (CFO) and to the Head of Credit Risk Management. Thereafter the Head of Credit should be allowed to delegate credit authority only to suitably qualified and experienced employees operating within the credit risk management organization or its sphere of influence.

2.11   POWER COLLECTIONS

The most effective way to obtain payment for most past due invoices is to simply ask your customer to pay. The sooner this is done, the better. The longer a receivable is outstanding, the less likely you are to receive payment. The probability of loss of a receivable is directly proportional to the time that has elapsed since delivery of the goods or services supplied.

Asking for payment of past due invoices is the quickest way to uncover any reasons for non-payment, such as non-receipt of the invoice or disagreement as to the price shown on the invoice. Customers are more likely to ignore a disputed invoice than to contact your company to sort out a query. Once you have dealt with any valid objections, payment normally materializes.

In the case of high-value invoices or documents presented to banks (under letters of credit (LCs), for example), arrangements should be in place to call the customer or bank three banking days before the due date, to ensure (a) your invoice has been received, (b) that the invoice is not disputed and (c) that payment will be made with value on the contracted due date.

In respect of low-value, high-volume invoices, automated or semi-automated arrangements should be made to block delivery of current and future orders, and to communicate with the customer without delay. Several service companies and software vendors offer solutions designed to deal cost effectively with high-volume, low-value, dispute resolution and past due receivables. Order-to-cash process outsourcing companies offer an alternative and effective way of dealing with high-volume business.

All past due invoices must be followed up promptly – as mentioned – and with persistent determination. Any queries or disputes must be dealt with expeditiously and excuses must be challenged with, for instance, requests for proof of payment instructions given or the imposition of deadlines. If delay continues all available means of leverage must be brought to bear to encourage the errant customer to pay. Forms of leverage to be considered include:

- Stopping current and future deliveries
- Negotiating a mutually acceptable settlement directly with the customer. This may include extended terms, with the provision of some collateral, for example
- Withdrawing the customer's credit limit
- Set-off of the past due receivable with any money due to the customer
- Requests for payment addressed directly to the Chairman or Chief Executive Officer, or holding company

- Realizing any collateral held by way of security
- Reporting the delinquent to credit reference agencies or trade associations
- Taking legal action to obtain a judgement and seize assets
- Sale of seized assets
- Petitioning for the bankruptcy of the customer

2.11.1   Specialized trade debt collectors and debt traders

A number of companies provide high-value international trade debt collection services. These services include: (a) "no cure no cost" services (you only pay a fee and related expenses if the collection effort is successful), (b) fee-based collection services and (c) debt purchase arrangements. It is often possible to sell past due trade debt at a discount, particularly sovereign debt (debt due by a government or a state-owned enterprise).

3

Country Risk

3.1 THE MISMANAGEMENT OF OOLRETAW

How one exporter survived and another didn't...

OSEx was bitter as he stared out of his apartment window at the cheap motel across the road. It was not just the dirty street scene that depressed him, day in and day out, nor was it the poor-quality coffee that was all he could afford, it was "country risk management" that overshadowed every day! It was memories of those corrupt incompetents who ran Oolretaw when his company was growing exports to that beautiful, resource-rich country. His local distributor was sound and such a great guy! He even paid every invoice in local currency, but a blocked bank account stuffed full of Ools was no use when OSEx's own creditors came calling!

Things had been going so well in Oolretaw that OSEx just hadn't noticed his buyer owed him the equivalent of 80% of OSEx's equity. When the crunch came OSEx's business just crumbled. Sadly his plans to retire to Seville and play golf crumbled along with his business! "Don't carry all your eggs in one basket" seems a trite saying but it's so apposite.

On the other hand, most days NSEx opens his blinds to allow bright sunshine to stream into his spacious living room. He stands for a moment drinking in the lush view of the fifth fairway. He often thinks of Oolretaw and how fortunate he was to have "country limits" in place long before it imploded in a stinking heap of corruption and theft. A lot of good people lost money that year and it was worse for the general population trapped in the country, so many wonderful people, so many good friends.

At least for NSEx's business the pain was shared with banks and insurance companies when the crunch came in Oolretaw. "Country risk management" can be a wonderful thing. No jobs were lost and no retirement plans had to be changed! Yes, that fifth fairway certainly looks inviting every day, and most days NSEx does not turn down the invitation.

The central idea behind country risk exposure management is that your company should be protected from destruction, in the event that any foreign country's credit power fails.

3.2 INTRODUCTION

Country risk is defined as the risk that something may happen in a foreign country that will stop or discourage *state-owned* and/or *privately owned* customers in that country from paying their debts on time.

It is usual to think of payment defaults as a result of a state-decreed moratorium on foreign payments, or a situation where assets are nationalized and foreign debts are no longer recognized (repudiated). However, a severe decline in the external value of a country's currency would equally cause all importers with payments due in foreign currency to face bankruptcy, and to default. Similarly a harsh tax introduced with retrospective application could convert many previously solvent companies into bankrupt companies.

3.2.1   Transfer or sovereign risk and local factors risk

Recovery or receipt of payment of a foreign receivable requires:

- Firstly, that the foreign currency exchange regulations of the foreign country allow the transfer of funds to be accomplished, and
- Secondly, that the foreign country has sufficient foreign currency available in its national treasury and banking system, or through international credit lines, to enable the necessary currency conversion.

The risk that one or other or both of these conditions will not be met, and therefore that a transaction will fail, is a division of country risk which is called *transfer risk* (if the buyer is privately owned) or *sovereign risk* (if the buyer is the state or a state-owned enterprise). This is the branch of country risk which banks and country risk consultancies (such as the Economist Intelligence Unit, Rundt's and Euromoney) have traditionally utilized their resources to analyse and forecast. This type of evaluation requires the employment of a specialized team of economists and political scientists, to analyse and report on social trends, economic data, political information and demographic statistics.

The second division of country risk may be called *local factors risk*. This includes all elements which could have a simultaneous negative effect on the financial well-being of many of the businesses operating in a particular country. These elements include, among other things:

1. The imposition of a new tax effective retrospectively.
2. The sudden drastic reduction in the external value of the domestic currency.
3. A natural disaster affecting the country's financial centre, such as a strong earthquake striking the Tokyo area.
4. The outbreak of rebellion or civil war.
5. A sharp rise in domestic interest rates.

There are several alternative and/or complementary ways to assess country risk, hence the comment "country risk assessment is an art and not a science" (Carter, 1987: 429).

However, all businesses that operate beyond the borders of their homeland need a systematic, cost-effective and practical internal process, designed to produce a quantitative monetary limit for their exposure to payment risk in each pertinent country.

3.3   COUNTRY RISK MANAGEMENT

Every company that is exporting goods or services will acquire country risk exposure. It is advisable to manage this exposure in order to ensure that your company will not become bankrupt if any one country fails. A country is said to have "failed" if your company's customers in that country are unable or unwilling to pay their debts due to your company. If a particular class of receivables were to be lost in this way, the loss would have to be covered by your shareholders' equity; if your equity were to be insufficient your company would face bankruptcy.

The situation in each country is dynamic and subject to rapid change. In addition countries are interdependent, so a change that affects one will affect many, often in different ways. Nevertheless changes are frequently subtle so it is necessary to be constantly alert. Positive changes are as important to note as negative changes, as they bring with them opportunities to do more business and to beat the competition.

Individual country limits should be reviewed formally at least twice every year and on an ad hoc basis if important developments occur. It is therefore imperative that a person or persons within your company be given the responsibility to undertake regular reviews, and to monitor developments in all relevant countries, on a daily basis. The latter task should be accomplished through giving attention to the news media, through conversations with agents, banks and colleagues, and through personal visits.

It is vital to gather information regularly as to your company's risk exposure in each country and to compare this with the country limits. This should be followed by action being taken to eliminate any exposure in excess of a particular country limit. Your company's accounting system must be designed to produce a regular report (perhaps weekly) which shows an analysis of receivables outstanding by country. If a particular receivable is guaranteed by a party resident in another country (a bank or parent company) the country designation of that receivable should be changed to the country of the guarantor. Other company exposures within countries could be added to such a report. Consignment inventory (stock) in a foreign country is an example of the type of exposure that could be added.

Comparing such a report to the country limits will highlight excess exposures so that action can be taken to transfer risks to other countries (by obtaining credit insurance or bank guarantees) or to redirect (limit) business activities. Action to eliminate excesses is the most important part of a country risk exposure management process, since it is in this way that a company's country exposures are actively managed.

3.4   COUNTRY RISK RATING AGENCIES

There are several internationally renowned agencies that produce regular country risk analysis reports and risk ratings, for subscribers. They generally employ teams of economists and political scientists to analyse countries on the following criteria:

- Economic indicators:
  - balance of payments
  - size of external debt
  - growth in GNP (gross national product)
  - inflation
  - debt servicing burden
  - structure of exports

- Political factors:
  - internal stability
  - external stability
  - the analyst's "sixth-sense factor"

Each agency coalesces its analysis down to a rating for each country and each agency has its own way of expressing such ratings. Some agencies assign a score out of, say, 10, others assign a letter or series of letters or a word, for example "substandard", others assign a combination of letters and numbers.

If the various agencies' ratings were used to rank a list of countries, the ranking would be similar for each agency, regardless of the variety of scoring methods used. This is so because all the agencies utilize similar data (data available publicly from sources such as the International Monetary Fund, World Bank and the Bank for International Settlements). Differences will arise where judgement has been applied particularly in assessing the skills of a country's officials in respect of economic management, and in assessing political factors.

It is conceivable that several ratings could be used to produce a combined or average rating for each country. However, it is unlikely that such an exercise would make sufficient difference to the overall outcome to justify the additional cost and effort involved. Hence it should be sufficient to choose any single recognized agency's risk ratings to serve as a base for your company's country risk analysis.

3.5   UNIQUE-COMPANY-PRODUCT-OR-SERVICE COUNTRY FACTORS

The country analysis and rating obtained from an agency report is clearly based on information available to all parties and therefore is not tailored specifically to the circumstances of your company. Consequently it is important to consider your company's unique position vis-à-vis each country, and to adjust your risk evaluation accordingly.

The following elements should be considered and each could be assigned a risk weighting, either positive or negative, depending on whether the element assessed is thought to reduce country risk or increase it, respectively. Elements to be considered:

- *The strategic position of your goods within the country being analysed.* Are your products vital for the maintenance of good order in the country, or for the maintenance of exports? Examples of such products are pharmaceuticals, fuel, fertilizer and food. Non-essential essentials, such as cigarettes and ingredients for beer manufacture, will be viewed similarly. Governments can be relied upon to ensure that debts due for essential and non-essential-essential goods are paid. However, non-essential goods (luxuries or goods with local substitutes) will carry a high risk of non-payment in a crisis.
- *Your company's influence with decision makers in the country.* If your company is in regular contact with decision makers in a country it will (a) have early warning of impending problems and (b) have a means to ensure that its interests, and those of other foreign creditors, are properly considered. This could reduce the country risk,

which is not only in your company's best interest but also in the long-term best interests of the host country.

- *Your company's strategy in the geographic area in question.* Your business may, for example, have a branch office operating in a neighbouring country but need to increase sales, in order to cover fixed office costs. This may require an easing of credit limits to assist the building of a regional market share. Hence you may be willing to tolerate more country risk than would otherwise be indicated by your analysis.
- *The strategy of your company's competitors.* In order to compete effectively with other suppliers your company may have to increase the amount of credit made available in a particular country.
- *The availability of payment risk cover from banks and/or the credit insurance market.* If country risk cover is available it may be possible to take on "excessive" risk, while limiting exposure to a country by using various risk sharing or limiting instruments, subject to payment of the cost of such loss protection.

3.6   A PRACTICAL COUNTRY RISK MANAGEMENT PROCESS

In Part III of this book (Chapter 10) you will find a power blueprint for practical country risk management.

4

Bank Risk

4.1 INTRODUCTION

"Bank risk" is the risk that a bank, which has added its name to a transaction, will fail to honour its commitment. A bank may "add its name to a transaction" by providing payment risk security in the form of a guarantee or a documentary credit (LC), or in various other ways.

When a bank provides security the "corporate risk of the buyer" is converted into "bank risk" for your internal control purposes. However, the bank's commitment to pay is *in addition to* the buyer's commitment to pay. Therefore, should the bank fail to honour its commitment, the seller still has the right to call upon the buyer to pay direct, in terms of the contract.

This is true even if the buyer has already paid the bank and given the bank instructions to transfer such payment to the seller. The bank acts as "the buyer's agent", so if the bank goes bankrupt while the payment is in process this loss must be borne by the buyer. This means that a buyer may have to pay twice if its bank fails. Refer to Figure 4.1 for an illustration of the contractual relationships involved.

Nevertheless, bank security is usually only obtained when the buyer's financial condition is not known, or when it is weak, or when the buyer has exceeded its credit limit with the seller. Alternatively, bank security may be used as a means of transferring the country risk exposure of a transaction from the buyer's country to the bank's country. Therefore it is vitally important for your company to assess the financial strength and business ethics of a bank *before* it is accepted as a "payment security provider".

The aim of such an assessment is to produce a list of acceptable banks, with each bank assigned a monetary limit for exposure management purposes.

4.2 WELL, WE HAVE THE BANK'S COMMITMENT BUT ARE WE SAFE?

Joe: (Dancing around his desk, waving a sheet of paper about) We're safe! We're safe! It's the LC! It's the LC! Here in my hand! Here in my hand!

Jim: (Mildly amused at this animated display of joy) Great! What's the name of the Opening Bank?

Joe: The what?

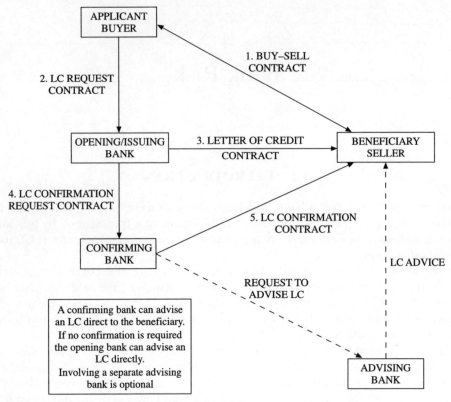

Figure 4.1   Letter of credit contractual relationships

Jim: Which bank sent us the letter of credit?

Joe: Oh. Hum. Oh here's the name, United Bank of Oolretaw. Sounds good?

Jim: Yes, sounds good, but is it good? That's the critical question.

4.3   UNDERSTANDING BANK RISK

Banks are generally highly leveraged entities. This means that they usually operate with a relatively small own equity and reserves base, compared to the debts and contingent liabilities which they incur on an ongoing basis. They are therefore vulnerable and could easily fail should either a large debtor customer fail or should they incur a large loss trading financial instruments. Other dangers lurk in respect of fraud, operational risk and country risk. The following examples will illustrate these points:

- The British bank *Barings* failed in 1995 due to overwhelming financial instrument trading losses, which were concealed from the supervisory authorities by fraud and alleged incompetence.

- More than 11 000 banks operate in the United States of America. Over the ten years 1980–89, 1077 *American banks failed or required rescue assistance* from the Federal authorities.
- The *Bank of Credit and Commerce International* (BCCI), which operated branches and subsidiaries in many financial centres worldwide, failed spectacularly in 1991, mainly due to the dishonesty of several senior executives.

Banks came into existence to perform the role of financial intermediaries, gathering together depositors' money and using it to finance economic activity in the community. This traditional role naturally led banks to have highly leveraged balance sheet structures, with relatively small capital amounts supporting much larger amounts due to depositors. Obviously banks utilize depositors' money to earn their income. This essentially vulnerable balance sheet structure is mainly supported by public trust. If trust in a bank's ability to pay on time is compromised it could quickly find itself in serious difficulty as depositors panic and rush to withdraw their funds. No bank can meet all its commitments immediately, bank balance sheet structures are built on the premise that not all depositors will act in unison to withdraw their money. Banks are organized to meet normal withdrawal demands only.

Given the inherent vulnerability of the banking system it is imperative that banks be properly managed and that the risks they accumulate are closely controlled by their executives. One important consideration, when assessing the reliability of a particular bank, is which bank supervisory authority exercises oversight in its case, and what standards that supervisory authority applies.

4.3.1 International bank supervision

In view of the key role that banks play in the economic fabric of every nation and the world, the Group of Ten (G-10) Central Bank Governors set up the Basel Committee of Supervisors in 1974 to enhance bank supervisory systems and prudential standards. This committee is also referred to as the Basle Committee, utilizing the French spelling of the city's name.

The Group of Ten originally consisted – mysteriously – of 11 countries: Belgium, Canada, France, Germany, Italy, Japan, the Netherlands, Sweden, Switzerland, the United Kingdom and the United States of America. Luxembourg and Spain joined the committee later, bringing the present representation to 13 countries.

The Basel Committee of Supervisors was established initially to address issues raised by the Herstatt and Franklin National Bank crises. The committee's task is to agree broad principles that will guide banking safety, banking soundness and reasonable competition standards. It meets four times each year on the premises of the Bank for International Settlements (BIS) in Basel, Switzerland. The BIS provides the secretariat for the committee, but the committee is not part of the BIS per se.

In July 1988 the Basel Committee of Supervisors published the *Basle Concordat*[1] (also called the Basel Capital Accord) which addressed three main concerns, namely the:

- Basis for convergence in the capital standards of major international banks

---

[1] References to the "Basle Concordat" and its history are largely based on Effros (1994: Ch. 19).

- Legal status of the branches of banks
- Bank supervisor's role in the prevention of money laundering

The Basle Concordat has since been amended and extended as the result of the lessons learnt from subsequent bank failures and banking crises. It provides the standard for *capital adequacy rules* which are applied in more than 100 jurisdictions worldwide. Capital adequacy rules are designed to ensure that:

- All banks which operate in such jurisdictions are being managed properly (that is that they are less likely to fail)
- Such banks are competing with each other on the basis of the same rules, even when operating across international borders

In terms of these rules banks are required to have a certain proportion of own funds, in relation to the amounts of various classes of obligations or liabilities that they undertake.

Implementation of the capital adequacy rules promoted by the Basle Concordat has been a major force promoting the increase of bank capital and reserves generally. Basle Concordat-based principles have also created a situation wherein no foreign banking establishment should escape supervision and such supervision should be of an adequate standard.

The Basel Committee of Supervisors has made a clear distinction between (1) *branches*, which have no separate legal status and are therefore integral parts of the parent bank, (2) *subsidiaries*, which are legally independent institutions owned by an entity incorporated abroad, and (3) *joint ventures*, which are legally independent institutions incorporated locally.

The Basle Concordat assumes that the solvency of a bank and its branches is indivisible. The opposite is true in respect of both subsidiaries and joint ventures. *Therefore any risk assessment related to subsidiaries or joint ventures should be independent of the risk assessment of the parent bank(s).*

4.3.2 Basel II

In January 2001 the Basel Committee issued a New Basel Capital Accord proposal, which will eventually replace the 1988 Basle Concordat. The intention is to refine and improve bank supervision, capital adequacy provisions, and risk measurement as it relates to minimum capital requirements.

The committee reviewed the New Basel Capital Accord on 10 July 2002, and a timetable for its implementation was agreed. The New Capital Accord will be finalized by the end of 2003 and implemented by the end of 2006. However, several large international banks are already taking steps to implement the provisions of the New Accord.

Basel II will be more flexible and appropriate to the task of the Basel Committee. Therefore it should improve the ability of the international banking system, and individual supervised banks, to withstand financial shocks in future.

4.4   BANK RISK ANALYSIS AND BANK EXPOSURE LIMIT DECISIONS

Every bank that provides your company with payment security (a guarantee or LC) or confirms an LC must be assessed as to its ability to meet its commitment. This is also true of any bank that is entrusted with company money or marketable securities, as investments or as collateral or for safekeeping. Your company's systems must be designed to produce a regular report (perhaps weekly) that shows an analysis of payment risk security outstanding by banks. Other company exposures to the listed banks, such as money market deposits, derivative transactions and/or forward foreign exchange contracts, should be added to this bank exposure report. Comparing this report against the internally approved bank limits will *highlight excess exposures* so that action can be taken to either transfer risks to other banks (by obtaining a second bank confirmation or counterguarantee) or to limit business activities.

The financial and management strength of each bank is dynamic and subject to rapid change. In addition, banks are interdependent so that a change that affects one will affect many, often in different ways. Nevertheless changes are often subtle so it is necessary to be constantly alert. Positive changes are as important to note as negative changes. Positive changes bring with them opportunities to do more business and to beat the competition. This may take the form of reducing the costs related to a series of transactions by eliminating the need to pay a second bank for *LC confirmations*, for example.

4.5   TWO PRACTICAL BANK RISK MANAGEMENT PROCESSES

In Part III of this book (Chapter 11) you will find two alternate power blueprints for practical bank risk management.

Risk Mitigation Power

5.1 INTRODUCTION

If your customer does not qualify for a credit limit or has exhausted its limit you should take steps to mitigate the payment risk or additional payment risk, respectively. However, you should always be sure your administration is of a high standard.

Most popular forms of payment or transfer risk security are not effective if your administration fails to fully meet the terms of the security contract. Invoices and the related documents (as required by the contract) must be accurate and must be produced on time. In addition the requirements associated with the specific risk mitigation instrument utilized must be scrupulously met.

Types of payment or transfer risk security include: payment in advance, credit insurance, letters of credit (LCs) (confirmed or not), bank guarantees, promissory notes (avalized or not), undisclosed risk sharing agreements or guarantees, documentary collections, parent company guarantees and credit derivatives.

5.2 CASH IN ADVANCE

Cash in advance (CIA) or cash with order seem at first glance to be simple and risk-free terms of sale. There are, however, several potential hazards that must be properly managed in order to ensure that losses are not incurred.

Where prices and/or quantities are uncertain, the preliminary invoices on which CIA payments are based will inevitably over- or underestimate the final invoice value. Thus a shortfall could arise, equating to the provision of unsecured credit, the very condition you are endeavouring to avoid. In the case of individual transactions it should be possible to contain any shortfall to a minimal amount. However, when delivering multiple orders in quick succession your administration may not be able to process final invoices fast enough to avoid significant amounts of exposure occurring.

Customers may demand some form of security to mitigate their risk in making payment before receipt of the goods. This would normally take the form of a bank payment in advance demand guarantee. A bank guarantee locks up an equal portion of your bank credit line and attracts a regular commission charge. It also invites a lesser known species of risk named "unfair calling risk" into your midst. Since payment under a demand guarantee can usually be triggered by the mere submission of a beneficiary's certificate that a specified event has occurred, it is possible for dishonest beneficiaries to obtain payment under guarantees. Insurance can be purchased to cover "unfair calling risk" at an additional cost, of course.

Buyers will inevitably expect some form of early payment discount in return for paying CIA. If agreed, such a discount will naturally reduce your gross sales margin, but can be justified if it is in line with the prevailing cost of funds. Unfortunately many early payment discounts are quoted in whole percentage points without giving attention to the per annum percentage cost of funds that is deduced. Hence one may see a 1% discount given for CIA when normal terms are 30 days after date of delivery, inferring a 12% per annum payment for the funds received early.

Discounts for early payment become part of the fabric of certain markets, allowing no scope for adjustment as interest rates move down. They are often well out of line with the cost of funds, amounting to a permanent impairment of gross margin.

5.3   CREDIT INSURANCE

Traditional credit insurance is structured on the same premise as other forms of insurance. Loss probabilities are calculated with reference to whole "populations" of debtors (ranging from good to bad risks) and premiums are levied on a "whole turnover" basis. The theory is that the premiums collected for providing cover on the good risks will enable the insurer to pay claims for failures in the "population".

This theory works fine for "fire and theft" type policies, for example, but in respect of "receivables" companies feel they can distinguish between "good" and "possibly bad" risks. Consequently they do not want to pay premiums to cover risks they feel sure will not materialize.

Credit insurers fix individual customer credit limits when providing "whole turnover" cover, and even stipulate risk mitigation requirements, such as LC support in some cases. This credit limit setting provision has been sold as a value added service by insurers, the claim being that companies minimize their need for in-house credit management resources and activities. However, many companies have found credit insurers' limits restrictive and uncompetitive. Some have persuaded their insurers to accept the company's own credit control processes and analysis skills as sufficient to avoid the imposition of insurer-determined customer limits. This only leads many to question the value added by "whole turnover" credit insurance.

The result of the two influences described is that some credit insurers have been driven to providing cover for "single" risks, be they corporate or sovereign. This has forced insurers to research and analyse credit risk, rather than relying on actuarial calculations, when deciding premiums and conditions. It should be noted that insurance providers ask companies covering single risks to contract to pay premiums over the whole contract period, based on the maximum exposure forecast, whether the business and exposure materialize or not. Additionally, companies are expected to pay between 70 and 100% of the total premium in advance. This has implications for the ultimate unit cost of credit insurance – particularly if there is a significant difference between forecast volumes and actual volumes delivered – and for cash flow.

There are still several other issues to consider in respect of credit insurance. Normally risk mitigation is structured on the basis that the protected party has to prove the agreed event has occurred in order to secure payment by the "seller of payment protection". In the case of insurance contracts, however, the enshrined approach is quite different. When an agreed event occurs the insurer undertakes an investigation into all the circumstances that have occurred during the life of the contract, to determine whether to pay or not. Bearing in mind that insurance contracts are based on obligations of "utmost good faith" and "minimization of loss" on the part of the insured, they often provide considerable "wriggle room" to enable the insurer to avoid paying a claim. Thus there is a significant element of uncertainty as to whether a claim will be paid or not in respect of credit insurance. It is impossible to know the outcome of a claim until (a) a loss event has occurred and (b) the subsequent investigation has been completed, at which time it is too late to seek alternative protection.

Moreover, all credit insurance policies provide for a "waiting period" before a claim will be paid. This period, usually from 180 to 360 days, runs from the time a loss occurs. Any money recovered in the meantime is set off against the amount to be paid by the insurer. Therefore credit insurance cannot meet the immediate cash needs of a company in the event a debtor fails to pay. If replacing that cash is vital to the short-term survival of your business, credit insurance will be virtually useless.

Only "virtually useless" because it may be possible to borrow funds on the strength of the fact that the unpaid receivable is insured. As a precondition your bank will want some assurance that the insurer will not "wriggle out" of its obligation. In other words, the uncertainty related to insurance payments may make it impossible to borrow or, at very least, will increase your cost of borrowing.

If the amount of an insured loss is significant, the sad fact is your company may be out of business by the time your insurer pays the claim. Nevertheless, some forms of credit insurance are easier to justify than others.

5.3.1 Export credit agency cover

Several countries maintain government-owned and/or subsidized credit insurance organizations. These usually have a restricted mandate allowing them to aid domestic industries by insuring sovereign, transfer and customer payment risks. This cover often includes pre-shipment or pre-delivery risk. If your company's exports qualify to be covered by an Export Credit Agency (ECA), taking such cover will normally make good commercial sense.

5.3.2 Pre-shipment or pre-delivery risk cover

Often companies have to incur significant costs preparing or manufacturing goods to fulfil orders, but the buyer's risk mitigation instrument (perhaps an LC) is only effective from the time of shipment. If goods are manufactured specifically for a particular buyer and/or pre-shipment costs incurred are significant, insurance may be the only way to mitigate the risk of loss should the buyer fail to perform prior to shipment. The buyer may fail to provide the required LC, in this example.

5.3.3 Country risk

Your customers in a particular country may be sound but you may feel that the underlying country risk is beyond your comfort level. In such a situation a policy covering country risk (commonly called "Political Risk" in the insurance market) could well add value to your operations.

5.3.4   Catastrophe cover

In cases where a company has excessive receivable exposures, in relation to its net tangible equity, it may be prudent to purchase "whole turnover" credit insurance with a significant "deductible". Having a large "deductible" (first portion of any loss for the company's account) will limit the cost of such insurance while providing protection for the company should a major loss occur.

5.3.5   Difficult markets

In addition to the usual credit insurance arrangements and techniques some companies set aside cash funds, taken out of current profit, in order to create a liquid reserve to cover potential bad debts. This enables such companies to relax credit policies and thereby to become more competitive, while ensuring financial survival. Two possible alternatives are (a) an external arrangement called *finite risk insurance* and (b) an *internal arrangement* managed within a group of companies.

Finite risk insurance (FRI)

FRI is based on an *investment policy* that is reinforced with a *credit insurance policy*, to cover any loss incurred before sufficient funds have been accumulated.

Example of a finite risk insurance arrangement

Given that a company decides that it wishes to:

- accumulate $15 million in cash reserves over a five-year period
- cover potential receivable losses
- have immediately available credit insurance protection up to $15 million

an FRI package will provide the company with:

- *An investment policy* designed to accumulate $15 million after five years, given fixed annual contributions (of, say, $2.6 million on the first day of each year) *plus* retained, compound investment income.
- *A linked insurance policy* which would provide cash to cover the difference between (a) the amount of any qualified receivable(s) lost and (b) the amount (if less) of the accumulated fund at the time the loss occurs, up to an aggregate of $15 million. Any such amount paid under the insurance policy would be repaid to the insurance company, as future annual contributions are paid over the remaining period of the agreement. Any investment income not earned/accumulated, as a result of a claim, would be a loss carried by the insurance company. Hence in this example the maximum at risk for the insurance company would be $2 million. This "timing and investment risk" is the difference between the total contributions of $2.6 million times 5 (= $13 million) and the FRI limit of $15 million. The insurance company would charge an appropriate premium for this cover, rolled into the agreed annual contribution.

Such an FRI arrangement would only cover losses up to a maximum aggregate

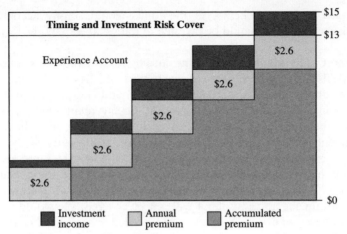

Figure 5.1   Finite risk insurance (five years)

amount of $15 million. If the full amount were to be lost on the first day of the arrangement, the insurance element would pay out immediately in full but the fund would have to be reimbursed over five years. The company would not enjoy any further "protection" from that particular arrangement but would have to continue making annual contributions for five years. Hence the loss would be written off over five years and the negative cash flow would be similarly spread. Conversely any amount in the FRI fund that is not needed to cover bad debts could be returned to the company at the end of the five-year period. Refer to Figure 5.1 for an illustration of this example.

Internal group-based arrangement

A "credit insurance" solution, based on a corporate group structure, could, for example, work as follows. The Group Credit Manager, based in Corporate Head-quarters, could operate a voluntary scheme for his business units. He could offer a credit insurance policy to his business unit managers – more simply worded than the usual commercial contract but covering the same key points. He could offer to cover 90% of commercial and country risk on those of the business unit's receivables that he has approved in terms of the policy agreement. In some cases he could stipulate security which must be obtained before cover could be effective. He could charge a "premium" based on normal commercial credit insurance rates. Such premium rates could be determined by simply asking a credit insurance company for a "ballpark" figure. The use of commercial premium rates should satisfy tax managers that the arrangement is not a "transfer of profit" scam. Internal credit insurance policies offered would be of the "whole turnover" type, covering the majority of receivables and stipulating a premium based on a percentage of total sales.

In due course the Group Credit Manager would receive claims when debts turned bad, she would pay out 90% (if a claim was valid in terms of the "policy"), so only 10% would go to the bottom line of the business unit at the time a receivable was written off. She would use premiums received to create a fund to use to cover any losses. This is not envisaged as a tax scheme, so the funds would simply accumulate on the corporate balance sheet and would be invested in the usual way by the Group Treasury department.

If the Group Credit Manager had some surplus funds available she could do "one off" special deals on specific higher-risk customers. In these cases she could write a policy to cover one account, on specific conditions, and charge a separate premium.

She could apply different criteria for credit management in each business unit, depending on the individual strengths of each unit. Some may have functioning credit departments with acceptable policies in place. In these cases she could review the credit policies and loss records, and set criteria and premiums accordingly. In other cases she herself could set credit limits and conditions for all customers, for instance when only a small number of customers are involved. Receivables that are not managed within the agreed criteria will not be covered; she would refuse to cover losses in cases where, for example, limits were exceeded or security was not obtained. In such cases 100% of any loss would go to the business unit bottom line, when the loss occurred.

It is recommended that tax and international commercial law advice should be obtained before such a structure is implemented.

5.3.6   Post-loss insurance

This type of cover cannot be described as a trade credit risk mitigation instrument, but it is a means of spreading the negative cash flow effect of a trade credit loss after it occurs. An explanation of post-loss insurance is included here in order to present in one place a complete list of the useful credit insurance products available.

Post-loss insurance can be described as follows:

- It is a loan "dressed up" as insurance.
- A company suffers a substantial bad debt loss for which it has made no provision.
- After suffering the loss it takes out an insurance policy (a) to cover the loss already suffered and (b) to cover some "future credit risks" that are very unlikely to occur.
- The insurance company then immediately pays the insured in full for the loss suffered. Thus the company does not have to suffer all of this loss in one year, neither as a deduction from profits nor as a negative cash flow.
- The company in turn pays premiums to the insurance company over, say, five years. The total of such premiums covers (a) the amount of the loss, (b) interest and (c) a very small premium for the risk of loss in respect of the "future credit risks" insured.
- The annual premiums are subsequently written off against profit when paid, as usual.
- In this way the company repairs both its cash flow and its year-to-year profit profile.
- Naturally if the company is "weak" the insurer may require some security to cover the premiums to be paid.

To shape this "loan" as a genuine insurance policy some "future risks" have to be rolled into the package. In order to do this cheaply the company would choose, for example, the risk of a loss exceeding a very high figure only on its AA or better rated counterparts.

5.4 LETTERS OF CREDIT UCP 500 AND eUCP

A Letter of Credit (LC) is a bank's *conditional* undertaking to pay a seller, provided certain documents with certain stipulated content are presented to the bank within certain other terms and conditions.

LCs are usually made subject to, and should only be accepted if they are subject to, the International Chamber of Commerce (ICC) Uniform Customs and Practice for Documentary Credits, 1993 Revision, ICC Publication Number 500. This is commonly referred to as *UCP 500* and has been in effect since 1 January 1994.[1]

UCP 500 provisions apply to all documentary credits (including to the extent to which they may be applicable, standby LCs) when they are specifically incorporated into the text of the credit. They are binding on all the parties to the credit, unless otherwise expressly provided in the credit.

Article 9a of UCP 500 makes clear that:

> An irrevocable Credit constitutes a definite undertaking of the Issuing Bank to pay, *provided* that the stipulated documents are presented to the Nominated Bank or to the Issuing Bank and that they comply with the terms and conditions of the Credit. (Abridged)

The *parties* to an LC are:

- *Applicant* = buyer
- *Beneficiary* = seller
- *Issuing or opening bank* – opens the LC for the buyer
- *Confirming bank* – guarantees the obligations of the issuing bank
- *Advising bank* – authenticates and advises a credit

The issuing, confirming and advising banks may be three separate banks. Alternatively, the issuing bank may also itself advise the LC, or ask an advising bank to do so, without confirmation. Likewise a confirming bank may also itself advise the LC. A bank that only advises an LC is only responsible to the beneficiary for the authenticity of the LC; in other words, for ensuring that the LC is properly issued by the named issuing bank, and properly confirmed by the confirming bank, if applicable.

Standby LCs usually incorporate simple documentary requirements, for instance the presentation of (1) a beneficiary's statement that the buyer failed to pay on due date, (2) a copy of the invoice, and (3) a copy of the proof of delivery document (bill of lading or railway bill, for example).

A standby LC is not meant to be utilized in the normal course of the related transaction(s). It merely stands by, waiting to be called upon (utilized) only in the event that the buyer fails to pay on due date. Most bank supervisors classify standby LCs as "financial guarantees" and therefore require banks to allocate more capital weighting to them (100% usually) than to self-liquidating trade-related transactional

---

[1] International Chamber of Commerce (ICC) publications are available from ICC Publishing SA, via its website: http://www.iccbooks.com.

or documentary LCs (20% weighting typically). This makes standby LCs more expensive than documentary LCs, in most jurisdictions.

Standby LCs can be issued under the International Standby Practices (ISP98) rules, instead of under UCP 500. See Section 5.5 below for details of this option.

5.4.1   Warning! Warning!

An LC is not an outright guarantee of payment; it is conditional, so there are three important risks to be borne in mind:

1. The *documentary risk* is the most significant risk. Documents presented to a bank for payment must comply with the conditions recorded in the LC and with international standard banking practice. Documents that are "almost the same as" or that "will do just as well as" are simply *not good enough* to ensure payment under an LC. If documents do not meet the conditions of the LC, the LC cannot be utilized to extract payment from the confirming bank and/or the issuing bank. Skill, knowledge, experience and meticulous attention to detail are all required of those preparing documents for presentation under LCs.
2. The *bank risk*. The risk that the bank will no longer be in business when it is time for it to pay. Refer to Chapter 4.
3. The *performance risk* relates to the risk that title (including the negotiable documents of title where applicable) will have passed to the buyer before an acceptable LC is in place. If the seller requires an LC to be amended after title has passed, the seller will be at the mercy of the buyer. LCs are irrevocable (unless otherwise stated) and therefore can only be amended with the explicit consent of all parties, applicant, bank(s) and beneficiary.

5.4.2   LC myths and legends

We have an LC so payment is assured.

NO. We have to meet every detail of the LC's conditions before payment can be assured.

The buyer is paying all the charges so the LC is costing us nothing.

NO. The buyer will factor such costs into its purchase decision, so the transaction will pay. Buyer and seller lose, only the banks gain.

In the case of a dispute, we will be able to predict the outcome by relying on an expert's interpretation of UCP 500.

NO. A number of high-profile disputes have been argued in court and several have produced judgements that have surprised (even horrified) the "experts".

5.4.3   LC reality

Most LC transactions are completed satisfactorily *not* because the instrument itself is effective, *only* because "the Applicant wants to pay".

A large part of the cost and administration effort involved in dealing with an LC is wasted because most sets of documents submitted to banks under LCs are discrepant.

That is, the documents do not conform to the requirements of the LC and therefore the bank is not obliged to pay.

The promised protection against "Applicants that do not want to pay" is, more often than not, a myth. All too often circumstances change around the delivery of contracted goods or services. For example, with the best of intentions an operator decides to load an extra tonne of product and with that your payment protection evaporates, since it is one tonne more than the maximum permitted in the related LC. A ship is delayed by bad weather and misses the latest permitted loading date. An airport is fogbound so your goods are delivered to a nearby airport and trans-shipped by road to their original destination, but the LC does not permit trans-shipment. These situations do not prejudice the buyer in any way but they do render the LC useless as a form of payment guarantee. When they happen it is too late to salvage the situation by arranging an amendment to the LC. This leaves you at the mercy of your buyer since it is seldom practical or cost-effective to retrieve your goods and sell them to another buyer.

5.4.4 LCs may be past their "use-by-date" but...

LCs may be past their "use-by-date" but they are still tremendously popular. Individuals and companies active in international trade are encouraged to use LCs. The ICC promotes an excellent distance learning course through which people can qualify as certified documentary credit specialists. Banks promote their documentary credit services, employing experts to process LCs and developing sophisticated systems to handle LCs more efficiently. The ICC achieved international agreement and published the first set of rules (Uniform Customs and Practice for Documentary Credits) in 1933. The UCP were revised in 1951, 1962, 1974, 1983 and again in 1993. Work has started on the sixth revision so UCP 600 will be published in due course. A Supplement to UCP 500 for electronic presentation (eUCP) – version 1.0 – was issued in January 2002. A manual defining for the first time international standard banking practice (ISBP) was published by the ICC in January 2003. In short there is a lot of vested interest, investment, infrastructure, history and tradition supporting the continuation of the key role played by LCs in international trade.

Nevertheless, LCs were originally developed in times when goods were transported by sea voyages that took many days, to far-off places that were difficult to access. LCs accommodated sell/buy transactions between strangers using the intermediary of their banks, which employed a relatively low-paid yet skilled workforce of document checkers. Times have changed and, admittedly, the UCP has changed to accommodate the changing technical demands of global trade and the increased diversity of thinking among the international trading community. However, it is difficult to avoid asking whether there is a better way to mitigate the credit risks inherent in international trade transactions.

Documentary credits (LCs) no longer pass the "cost versus benefit" test in the contemporary context for many companies. They are simply too:

- Labour and expertise intensive
- Expensive
- Difficult to process correctly and quickly
- Unpredictable
- Involved with many intermediaries

In complete contrast to this, companies want risk mitigation instruments that:

- Will pay unequivocally, should a buyer fail to pay an invoice on the due date
- Provide for rights and duties that are certain in law
- Provide good value for money
- Can be established and processed quickly

5.4.5   Alternatives for high-volume, low-value transactions

TradeCard is an alternative that offers similar risk mitigation qualities for relatively low-value transactions (around US$100 000 each in value), with several advantages. Intermediaries (banks) are eliminated from the process, electronic documents are automatically checked for acceptability and authenticity, and invoice settlement is automated. Refer to Section 7.3 for details.

Cash in advance may be another viable alternative depending on the circumstances – see Section 5.2 above.

5.4.6   Alternatives for low-volume, high-value transactions

Payment undertakings with *risk sharing agreements* offer a viable alternative, provided the size and/or repetitive nature of the transactions justify the initial investment in time and legal costs required to negotiate an agreement with a bank. Refer to Chapter 13 for details.

5.4.7   Supplement to UCP 500 for electronic presentation (eUCP) – version 1.0

eUCP has been designed to be used in conjunction with the current Uniform Customs and Practice for Documentary Credits (UCP 500) and any later revision. It describes rules necessary to enable the presentation and processing of electronic documents, or a mixture of electronic and paper documents, in practice.

5.4.8   Warning! Buyers beware!

You may provide documentary credits (LCs) when buying goods, either because the seller insists or in order to ensure that you receive title to (ownership of) the goods at the same time as the seller is paid. Beware because LCs are about documents only, not about goods. UCP 500 Article 4 provides:

> In Credit operations all parties concerned deal with documents, and *not* with goods, services and/or other performances to which the documents may relate.

Therefore forged documents may be presented and the bank will nevertheless be obliged to pay, if they conform to the LC requirements and the bank is not aware of the fraud being perpetrated. Likewise the goods actually shipped/received may not meet the specifications required by your purchase order or those noted in the documents presented to the bank. Sadly you will probably only discover this type of fraud after the bank has paid your supplier.

The examples of *fraud risk* described here serve to emphasize the absolute necessity to undertake *due diligence investigations* in respect of every counterparty, as well as to point out additional limitations related to the venerable LC.

5.5   STANDBY LETTERS OF CREDIT SUBJECT TO ISP98

International Standby Practices 1998 (ISP98), ICC Publication 590, were formulated under the auspices of the Institute of International Banking Law and Practice Inc., in association with the International Chamber of Commerce (ICC). This work was undertaken because it was clear that while many workable standby LCs are opened under UCP 500 rules, the latter are not fully applicable nor entirely appropriate to the issuance of standby LCs. This is particularly the case in respect of non-commercial and complex standby LCs. A standby LC, or other similar undertaking, may be made subject to ISP98 rules simply by recording within the standby LC that it is "subject to ISP98".

Commercial transactions have, for the most part, been satisfactorily covered by standby LCs subject to UCP 500 since 1993, so the majority of such standby LCs issued today are still made subject to UCP. Nonetheless the ISP98 rules are – in respect of standby LCs of any kind – far superior to those provided in UCP 500. ISP98 leaves fewer unanswered questions in relation to situations that may arise during the life of a standby LC and, as such, remove more elements of uncertainty from related scenarios. Predictability, and balanced but clear definitions of rights and responsibilities, are the hallmarks of a superior risk mitigation tool. ISP98 is designed to provide these qualities in relation to standby LCs.

Naturally a standby LC subject to ISP98 (an ISP98 standby) should only be accepted after the ISP98 rules have been studied and found to be acceptable, within your company.

5.6   BANK GUARANTEES AND UNIFORM RULES FOR DEMAND GUARANTEES (URDG)

Guarantees obtained to mitigate customer payment risk must be considered on the basis of the specific text contained within the document. All guarantees should be irrevocable. Assuming that the guarantor is an acceptable risk for the amount guaranteed, and noting that it is prudent to take legal advice, there are usually four important aspects to consider in respect of guarantees, whether governed by URDG or not.

Firstly, is the obligation of the guarantor separate and independent from that of your customer? You should not be obliged by the terms of the guarantee to first sue your customer before claiming payment from the guarantor. Moreover the guarantor should agree to pay upon receipt of a demand, without any set-off or counterclaim.

Secondly, which country's law is applicable to the guarantee and what are the provisions of the law regarding demand guarantees? Most guarantees are stated to be subject to the laws of the country in which the guarantor has its place of business. In any event it is advisable to investigate the nuances of the applicable law in relation to any guarantee. This in order to keep to a minimum the surprises that would otherwise only surface when you make a claim for payment under the guarantee.

Thirdly, is your company capable of meeting the terms and conditions of the guarantee (without relying on its guaranteed customer to supply any necessary document(s) or authorization) within the time limits specified in the guarantee?

Fourthly, is your company permitted to vary the terms and conditions of the underlying contract by mutual agreement with the guaranteed customer from time to time, without advising or obtaining the prior permission of the guarantor? It is important that this right be available to your company, in order to avoid inadvertently nullifying the guarantee.

Note that guarantees, as ancillary contracts, must be given in exchange for "consideration", that is for something of value, be that the payment of a fee (even a token fee) or be it your agreement to provide trade credit in future. Trade credit already provided will probably not qualify as "consideration". Failure to prove the provision of consideration will render a guarantee unenforceable, unless it was executed as a "contract (or deed) under seal":

> a contract that does not require consideration in order to be binding but that must be sealed, delivered, and show a clear intention of the parties to create a contract under seal. (definition by "FindLaw" at http://www.findlaw.com)

5.6.1   URDG

Guarantees issued subject to the URDG, ICC Publication 458, will incorporate best international practice provisions, balance the interests of the parties, and avoid some of the common abuses that otherwise plague such obligations.

The URDG were first published by the ICC in 1992, but have not been widely adopted. This lack of take-up of the URDG is difficult to understand in that they consist of a set of sensible, well-balanced and relatively simple rules. It is important to note that each article and subarticle can be excluded from applicability to a particular guarantee, at the option of the parties, by mutual agreement. Therefore any provision in URDG that does not fit the circumstances, or causes some offence, can simply be excluded from the terms of the relevant guarantee. Most of the provisions cover the usual, so-called, boilerplate provisions of guarantees that are payable upon presentation of a simple demand. Hence a lot of legal drafting and argument can be avoided by adopting the URDG provisions.

In terms of URDG any entity can issue a demand guarantee; the rules are not limited to guarantees issued by banks or insurance companies. A demand guarantee subject to URDG should only be accepted after the URDG rules have been studied and found to be acceptable, within your company. A method of effectively securing receivables employing demand guarantees is fully described in Chapter 12.

5.7   PARENT COMPANY GUARANTEES

A parent company guarantee (PCG) or sibling company guarantee is generally only as "good" as the ethics of the management of the group of companies. Ironically, if the ethics within a group are good it will be worthwhile obtaining a PCG but it will be unnecessary. On the other hand, if the ethics are bad it will be essential to take a PCG but the PCG will most likely be useless. In cases where you are uncertain whether the holding company is aware of a transaction, obtaining a PCG will remove any doubt.

It is always necessary to analyse the creditworthiness of the parent or sibling company offering a guarantee. If the prospective guarantor has assets of its own (not least among these could be its reputation and/or brand assets) a guarantee commitment can be given some credence. If, however, the guarantor is a pure holding company merely owning shares (stock) in its subsidiaries and receiving dividend income only, little value can be placed on the separate undertaking to pay embodied in a guarantee.

In some countries, Germany, the Netherlands and the Republic of Ireland, for example, holding companies are either obliged to "guarantee" the liabilities of their "consolidated" subsidiaries or can publicly register an undertaking to "guarantee" the liabilities of particular subsidiaries. Care should be exercised and legal advice obtained, should you wish to rely upon such engagements. Some such arrangements, for instance, are subject to annual renewal so could fall by the wayside without this fact coming to your notice until it is too late.

In many jurisdictions, such as the Federation of Russia, the currency controller (normally the central bank) considers corporate guarantees in favour of non-residents to represent the potential export of "capital" funds, as opposed to "trade"-related payments. In such cases provision of corporate guarantees to non-residents requires central bank approval and that is either merely difficult and time-consuming to win, or impossible to obtain.

Any PCG must be carefully drafted in order to ensure the guarantor's obligation is separate and independent from that of your customer. You should not be obliged by the terms of the guarantee to first sue your customer before claiming payment from the guarantor. The terms of the PCG should also permit you to vary the terms and conditions of the underlying contract by mutual agreement with the guaranteed customer from time to time, without advising or obtaining the prior permission of the guarantor. It may be advisable to make PCGs either subject to the URDG, or subject to the International Standby Practices 1998 (ISP98) rules.

Despite careful drafting, the amount of reliance placed on a PCG must always be tempered by the realization that the holding company executive will be in a position to reorganize and redistribute assets to frustrate your claim, should they wish to avoid their guarantor obligations.

5.7.1 Transactional parent or sibling company guarantees

Customers may prefer to restrict the applicability of any required PCG or sibling company guarantee to a related individual contract or transaction. This will likely increase the related administrative burden (handling cost and documentation risk) since it will lead to an increase in the number of guarantees received. Each guarantee will have to be checked to ensure it complies with your company's requirements, and that it matches the details of the applicable transaction. In addition each related transaction will have to be carefully monitored and controlled, to ensure that it is and remains covered by the terms of the related guarantee.

5.7.2   Letters of comfort

These only confirm that your customer is a subsidiary within the group, and that the holding company is aware of your customer's obligations. A letter of comfort's value can be enhanced if the holding company is willing to additionally undertake to inform you of any material change in the ownership of its subsidiary.

5.8   PAYMENT UNDERTAKINGS AND RISK-SHARING AGREEMENTS

The payment undertaking based risk-sharing agreement method of mitigating payment risk offers a viable and flexible alternative to the use of both documentary credits (including standby LCs) and bank guarantees.

Payment undertakings are sometimes called purchase confirmations. They ask no more of the buyer than a simple but separate confirmation that the buyer will fulfil the terms of its contract with the seller. A payment undertaking does not impose any additional burden upon the buyer. The buyer is not expected to undertake to do anything over and above that already agreed in the purchase/sale contract. A payment undertaking is, however, a separate formal irrevocable document, usually addressed directly to a bank designated by the seller.

In preparation for this type of arrangement the relevant purchase/sale contract must contain the following two clauses:

Credit: At least five days prior to delivery Buyer will send to Seller's bank, with a copy to Seller's financial contact, a payment undertaking in a format acceptable to Seller (bank details and payment undertaking text will be provided).

and

Assignment: This agreement will not be assignable by either party without the written consent of the other, which shall not be unreasonably withheld. However, in the event payment is not made by the Buyer on due date, Seller has the right to assign the financial rights under this agreement to a bank without the prior consent of the Buyer.

5.8.1   Historical development of payment undertakings

Businesses that specialize in oil trading (traders) usually have a limited financial asset or capital base since their main assets are the skills and contacts of their executives. They therefore had difficulty establishing significant documentary credit facilities with international banks.

When a trader participated in "back-to-back" deals (see box) in terms of which, for instance, it bought a cargo of crude oil from an oil producer that required it to provide documentary credit (LC) payment security, a mechanism was needed to enable an international bank to open the LC for the trader. Normally the trader would immediately sell the same cargo to a highly creditworthy oil company (oil major), but since the oil major (ultimate buyer) would not normally provide an LC in favour of the trader, a bank could not operate a traditional "back-to-back" LC arrangement. Hence an alternative mechanism was needed to enable a bank to open the necessary LC for the trader.

A *"back-to-back" LC arrangement* is one in terms of which a bank opens an LC that emulates the terms and conditions of an LC received by its customer. The terms and conditions of each must be sufficiently similar to enable the bank to reimburse itself, when it has paid out under its own LC, by presenting documents and collecting payment under the received LC. The bank handles all the documents related to both transactions and thereby secures its position, provided no mistakes are made in the text of its own LC and/or in handling the related documents. In this way the bank incurs "documentary risk" rather than "customer payment risk" and is therefore able to open LCs for financially weak customers that act as intermediaries.

Some international banks found a way to do this using payment undertakings and consequently assisted in the expansion of international trade, and in the safe expansion of their own business activity. This is achieved by asking an oil major (ultimate buyer) to issue a payment undertaking direct to the trader's bank, irrevocably undertaking (a) to pay for the cargo, if it is delivered as agreed in the purchase/sale contract, and (b) to route the payment directly to the account of the trader at that specific bank, provided the trader's invoice contains details of that specific bank.

This simple device enables the LC issuing bank to control the receipt of the funds from the oil major and the payment to the seller (producer) under the LC, utilizing those same funds less the trader's gross margin. This permits such banks to open LCs that they could not otherwise open.

The use of the payment undertaking methodology has since been expanded to provide an alternative method of covering general payment risk where no intermediary parties (traders) are involved. It has, for example, proved popular in relation to buyers situated in the Czech Republic, Hungary, Poland, Nigeria and Angola, as an alternative which is more flexible and cost-effective than the use of either documentary credits or bank guarantees.

Using the payment undertaking method banks now cover (underwrite) direct corporate payment risk through agreements with sellers. Such agreements are generally not disclosed to the buyers, but the buyers are required to provide payment undertakings. In some cases the seller formally assigns the proceeds of the sale to the bank before delivery of the contracted goods or services. In these cases the buyer is asked to acknowledge the assignment of proceeds. A bank's charge for covering payment risk in this manner is borne by the seller.

5.8.2 Payment undertakings and risk sharing in practice

In Part III, Chapter 13, you will find a detailed description of the payment undertaking process and examples of related documentation.

5.9 DOCUMENTARY COLLECTIONS

Documentary collections are managed on the basis of the Uniform Rules for Collections (ICC Publication 522) which are widely accepted internationally. There are three variations on the documentary collection theme, and each provides an element of payment risk mitigation. However, if your company utilizes this form of mitigation you will always face the danger that your goods will arrive at their destination before your customer has paid or made a commitment to pay. Therefore you will risk having a distressed (refused) cargo languishing in a foreign port, accumulating storage and other costs. Buyers have often used such situations to reopen price negotiations, particularly when commodity prices have dropped (relative to the original contract price) and/or when the seller is unable to find an alternative buyer in the destination region and the potential freight cost does not justify recovery of the goods.

The three variations on collection terms mentioned are documents against payment, documents against acceptance, and documents against bank guaranteed acceptance. In all cases commercial documents (invoice, packing list and bills of lading, for example) and/or financial documents (bill of exchange or promissory note) are sent to the buyer's bank, either through your bank and its correspondent bank in the buyer's country or direct. The documents are accompanied by a letter requesting the buyer's bank to handle them in accordance with the Uniform Rules for Collections (URC 522) and your instructions. Your instructions will be framed in accordance with the terms applicable to the transaction. If the presenting bank accepts the collection request it becomes responsible for carrying out your instructions.

5.9.1   Documents against payment (DP)

In the normal course you would dispatch the goods, gather the related documents and send the documents to the presenting bank with instructions to "release the documents to the buyer against payment". In this way you ensure that the buyer only receives the documents in exchange for payment. The URC require the presenting bank to inform you promptly if the buyer fails to "take up the documents", or to remit the funds to you without delay. In this way you retain control of the goods until payment is made. If the documents are not "taken up", that is if payment is not made, in theory you can recover the documents (and the goods) and redirect the goods to a new buyer.

In practice the presenting bank will often release the documents "in trust" to its customer (the buyer) to enable the latter to examine them prior to payment. The presenting bank does this at its own risk. If its customer subsequently takes possession of the goods but does not pay, the presenting bank will be obliged to pay.

5.9.2   Documents against acceptance (DA)

This is the same as a DP collection except for the fact that a financial document will be included in the package sent to the presenting bank. The financial document (a bill of exchange or promissory note) will stipulate the terms of payment agreed in the contract of sale. The related instruction letter will usually request the presenting bank to release the commercial documents to the buyer against "acceptance" of the financial document. Alternatively it is permissible (but not normally practical when a credit period is allowed) to instruct the presenting bank to obtain acceptance of the financial document but only to release the commercial documents against payment. The presenting bank will subsequently hold the accepted instrument and present it for payment on your behalf, upon its maturity.

The advantage of obtaining an accepted promissory note or bill of exchange before releasing the commercial documents is that in most parts of the world these instruments are easy to discount (sell) without recourse. They are also easier to prosecute should they be dishonoured by non-payment.

5.9.3 Documents against bank guaranteed acceptance (DA*)

This is the same as a DA collection except that you request the buyer's bank to guarantee that the buyer's payment will be received. In order for this request to be effective it is preferable to include a document setting out the text of the guarantee requested, with the collection instruction. In this way, or by specific instructions addressed to the presenting bank, you must make it clear that you require the bank's separate undertaking to pay, as opposed to an ancillary guarantee. Payment under an ancillary guarantee could be refused should some dispute be raised in relation to the underlying contract.

5.10   CREDIT DERIVATIVES

Unfortunately credit derivatives as they have been structured for use by banks and investment funds – formalized by the International Swaps and Derivatives Association (ISDA) – are not appropriate for use in relation to the vast majority of trade credit payment risks. The main inhibitor to the use of credit derivatives is "basis risk", that is the lack of correlation between the changes exhibited by the "reference asset" of a credit derivative and the changes exhibited simultaneously by the receivable asset you are trying to protect. In addition the "specified credit events" that would trigger a credit derivative do not always match the delinquency (late payment) or default (failure to pay) events specific to your trade receivable.

The type of credit derivative that is most likely to be considered in the context of active trade credit risk mitigation is the credit default swap (CDS).

5.10.1   Credit default swaps (CDSs)

A CDS is a contract in terms of which one party (the purchaser of default protection) undertakes to pay the other (the seller of default protection) a fee for protection against the occurrence of one or more specified events in relation to a third party, called the "reference party". If one or more of the specified events occurs – as evidenced by publicly available information – the seller of default protection will pay compensation to the buyer of protection either through "physical" or "cash" settlement.

It is important to note at this point that the requirement that a specified event must be evidenced by publicly available information restricts the range of "reference assets" that can be cited in a CDS to publicly traded instruments such as bonds. Hence if your customer has issued publicly traded debt instruments, perhaps Eurobonds, you could buy a CDS that would be triggered if those Eurobonds, for example, are subject to one or more of the following events: failure to pay, bankruptcy or insolvency, adverse debt rescheduling, cross-default or debt repudiation.

If a trigger credit event occurs during the term of a CDS that calls for *physical settlement*, you will be required to assign or sell the reference asset (your customer's Eurobonds) to your counterparty (the payment risk protection provider). That is, Eurobonds with a face value equivalent to the notional amount of trade credit exposure protection purchased. Your counterparty will be obliged to take the reference assets offered and pay you the par or face value in return. It is unlikely you would actually own any of the reference asset, so you would face the prospect of having to purchase the reference asset in order to realize your CDS protection. If many CDS holders are attempting the same activity concurrently, you could face the bizarre situation of the price of the failed reference Eurobonds rising as holders compete to obtain assets to "put" to their counterparties.

The other issues to be considered in this example situation are, firstly, while they negotiate a rescheduling of their commitments related to debt instruments, such as Eurobonds, customers are likely to continue paying trade debts related to goods required to maintain ongoing company activities. Hence you could receive a "windfall" payment without suffering any actual loss. Secondly, if you do suffer a loss related to your trade receivable, it is unlikely that the amount of compensation you receive via the settlement of the related CDS will accurately match the magnitude of your loss.

If this example was subject to *cash settlement* when triggered, your counterparty payment risk protection provider would simply pay you the difference between the post-default cash value of the reference asset (Eurobond) and the par value.

Obviously, if your customer does not issue any publicly traded debt instruments the only way to utilize the CDS mechanism to mitigate trade credit risk is to choose an unrelated reference asset. This would amplify the basis risks described in the preceding paragraphs. The possibility that your customer could default without the CDS being simultaneously triggered would be the most serious and prescient risk.

5.11   NETTING AGREEMENTS

Netting (set-off) involves effectively using your company's own credit standing to reduce its exposure to a customer. Netting can only be effective in situations that involve buying and selling between the same two legal entities.

There are four common types of netting, viz.:

- *Settlement netting*, which is effective only in respect of items of the same kind due on the same day. It is only operative on the mutual due date.
- *Novation netting*, in terms of which only like classes of transaction with the same settlement dates may be set off against each other. Novation netting takes effect each time a subsequent transaction is entered into. This does reduce payment risk but it does not provide for netting in the case of a default by one of the parties.
- *Close-out netting*, which stipulates that if there is a default by either party all mutual transactions will be closed and set off immediately. This is the most popular form of netting.
- *Multilateral netting* in practice is not generally effective in most jurisdictions, outside of special clearing house systems.

The effective administration of netting arrangements is costly because it requires the intensive involvement of highly qualified people and the utilization of expensive information systems. It also carries considerable "documentation risk". That is the risk that the related documents will not be accurate or complete and therefore a set-off claim will fail.

When effecting a netting close-out, it is extremely difficult to ensure all transactions are valued correctly and in real time. Hence it is easy to miss some small losses or bonus gains on a close-out.

The negotiation of netting documentation often proves to be time-consuming and arduous. Negotiations based on ISDA framework documentation are no exception because a general lack of standardization of requirements creates scope for debate between the parties.

5.12   COLLATERAL SECURITY

In some sectors of business it is usual for debtors to utilize assets to mitigate the credit risk they pose, and thereby persuade their counterparties to provide transaction-based credit. This practice is, for the most part, confined to the banking and derivatives trading sectors.

Collateral generally takes one of two possible forms, the first being a *security interest* in an asset. The second form of collateral is the *outright transfer* of ownership of an asset.

5.12.1   Security interest

This is usually a pledge, charge, mortgage, lien or hypothecation. It is advisable to be wary (a) of the possible existence of negative pledges given by the counterparty, (b) of perfection requirements for security interests and (c) of the possible effects of fluctuations in the pledged asset's value.

A "negative pledge" is an undertaking that a debtor (borrower) gives to a lender not to pledge any of its assets to third parties, without the permission of the lender. The existence of a negative pledge may make your attempt to establish a security interest ineffective.

Creditors often need to observe certain legal requirements and subsequently register their rights in order to perfect (successfully complete) the creation of a security interest. Failure to meet statutory requirements could render a security interest void.

5.12.2   Outright transfer

In some circumstances the most efficient way to "perfect" collateral security is by transferring ownership of the collateral assets into the name and possession of the creditor. This creates an obligation on the transferee to return assets of the same type (but not necessarily exactly the same assets as originally delivered) when the obligations of the transferor have reduced to zero (as a result of intervening price movements) or have been repaid.

The value of the transferred assets will be set off against the debtor's obligations under the contract, if a transferor defaults. In respect of mutual marked-to-market collateral cover agreements (say the transfer of marketable securities) it is important to guard against finding your company in the position where it is obliged to transfer its securities to a less creditworthy counterparty. This may come about as a result of a change in the underlying transaction's value, when a mutual transaction moves "out of the money" from your perspective. Should the position later reverse, and your counterparty subsequently be tardy in returning collateral and become bankrupt before rebalancing the position, your company could lose the excess collateral and the profit on the trade.

5.13   BILLS OF EXCHANGE AND PROMISSORY NOTES

Promissory notes (PNs) form a subset of bills of exchange in that they are covered by the same laws and rules, except only one party is needed to create a PN. A bill of exchange must be created through the actions of two signing parties, the party wishing to be paid and the party being asked to pay. Bills of exchange and PNs are also known as "drafts".

A PN subject to English law and jurisdiction – that is to say, subject to the Bills of Exchange Act 1882 – is defined as:

> An unconditional promise in writing, made by one person to another, signed by the maker, engaging to pay, on demand, or at a fixed or determinable future time, a sum certain in money, to, or to the order of, a specified person, or to bearer.

A PN has the advantage of being a separate and unconditional undertaking to pay on a certain date. Therefore it cannot later be disputed on grounds related to any underlying contractual relationship, including a contract for the provision of goods or services. This quality can serve to partly mitigate payment risk, in that it is easy to evidence failure to pay a PN and to obtain a judgement accordingly. The latter will assist collection activity by, for example, making it possible to seize the assets of your customer to satisfy the debt.

The inherent qualities of a PN also make it readily marketable through endorsement and discounting. However, you should bear in mind that if your company endorses a PN it becomes liable to any subsequent "endorser that is required to pay" or the "holder in due course" of that PN, should the maker (your customer) fail to pay. In order to avoid this liability it is necessary to annotate any such endorsement with words such as "without recourse to us".

The barrier to using PNs to alleviate payment risk is customers' reluctance to sign PNs prior to receipt of the goods supplied. Therefore you will normally only be provided with a PN either (a) through the documentary collection process, when it will be exchanged for the commercial documents, or (b) as part of your contracted payment terms, in response to receipt of your invoice and after the goods have been examined. Hence in most cases PNs are useful from the point of view of discounting (selling) receivable amounts – thereby assisting your firm's liquidity and return on assets – but they are not particularly useful as payment risk mitigants.

The Bills of Exchange Act 1882 is applicable in the United Kingdom, and in the

Republic of Ireland where it has been adopted almost word for word. The 1882 Act has also provided the model for local legislation in most Commonwealth countries. PNs may alternatively be created subject to the laws of states that have ratified the Geneva Conventions of 1930 (including the Geneva Uniform Law on Bills of Exchange and Promissory Notes of 1930). These include most other European countries and many in Asia. The Geneva Uniform Law has also provided the model followed by many of the states that have not adopted the United Kingdom paradigm, even though they have not ratified the 1930 Conventions. This includes the People's Republic of China.

The Russian Federation and other members of the Commonwealth of Independent States still apply the law on bills of exchange of the former USSR, enacted on 7 August 1937. Bills of exchange and PNs are referred to as "Veksels" in the Russian Federation.

The Uniform Commercial Code (UCC) regulates bills of exchange and PNs in the United States of America.

A method of effectively securing receivables employing PNs is fully described in Chapter 12.

5.14   DISCOUNTING RECEIVABLES AND FORFAITING

Discounting receivables (selling them at less than their face value, without recourse) and forfaiting[2] (selling bank guaranteed bills of exchange or PNs at less than their face value, without recourse) are only payment risk mitigating actions to the extent that they enable early receipt of payment. This is the case because you hold no payment security at any time between the moment of delivery and the moment of receipt of cash from the forfaiter. Hence, although payment risk is not mitigated by this means, forfaiting shortens the period of credit exposure. This is welcome because in theory – strongly supported by practical experience – the longer a receivable is outstanding after delivery of the related goods or services, the less likely it is to be paid.

Discounting a receivable effectively transfers the payment risk to a bank for the remainder of the receivable's life, and reduces the related cash cycle dramatically.

Note that it is possible, though not customary, to eliminate payment risk exposure identified above by enhancing a forfaiting transaction. This can be accomplished by obtaining a PN from your buyer before delivery of the goods, based on a proforma invoice. However, this requires a great deal of trust on the part of the buyer, because the PN creates a separate buyer obligation not inherently related to the buy–sell contract. Therefore, should you fail to deliver the goods you could nonetheless present the PN for payment. Refer to Chapter 12 for details of an appropriate process.

Discounting of receivables and forfaiting are useful ways to recycle limited credit lines by freeing them up to cover subsequent deliveries. This is particularly so in markets where extended credit terms are usual. Hence if you are comfortable with a certain level of credit risk but want to deliver additional goods or services that would otherwise cause excessive exposure, you can discount the existing receivable to make credit available.

---

[2] The term "déclarer forfait" in French means to surrender or forfeit a right. Hence the use of the word "forfait" in relation to the discounting of receivables, which is the act of giving up the right to be paid.

Forfaiting was originally developed to support German machinery and equipment exports to the countries of the former Soviet Union in the 1970s. It was used as a means of managing medium- to long-term finance, six-month to seven-year terms. Often the risk was underwritten (guaranteed) by export credit agencies (ECAs) – government-owned export credit insurers – as well as by the buyer's bank. Today it is increasingly common for forfaiting facilities also to cover short-term credit (as short as 30 days) and to be undertaken by forfaiters (mostly international banks) without the support of ECAs, credit insurers or other banks, simply on the strength of the buyer's credit worth and a favourable country risk assessment.

Cost is an important consideration in respect of receivables discounting or forfaiting. On the one hand the forfaiter is buying a self-liquidating debt in a tradable form, on the understanding that the goods supplied will generate revenue to provide the source of repayment. On the other hand, the forfaiter must bear the payment risk of the buyer, transfer risk of the buyer's country, and the exchange risk of the buyer's home currency. In most cases the cost to your company of obtaining immediate liquidity by selling receivables will be higher than the cost of borrowing funds directly in your company's own name. In addition, where a bank guarantee or aval is required, your buyer will have to carry that cost. Therefore, if alternative payment risk mitigation methods are available they should be fully investigated. It may well be possible to generate a competitive all-in price advantage or increase net revenue from a sale if the alternative proves to be cheaper.

The cost of forfaiting consists of several distinct layers, viz:

1. The cost of funds. That is the cost to the forfaiter of the cash paid to you before money can be collected from your buyer. This will usually be related to the inter-bank offered rate available in the relevant currency market.
2. The cost of the "own capital" the forfaiter must allocate to the transaction.
3. The cost of hedging any currency risk, through a forward sale of the currency to be collected from your buyer on the PN due date. This usually relates to the interest rate differential apparent between the home markets of the respective currencies.
4. The "credit spread" (margin indicated by the relative credit rating) of the buyer or guarantor bank.
5. The "credit risk premium" (margin indicated by the relative perceived risk) applicable to the buyer's or guarantor's country transfer risk.
6. The forfaiter's positive or negative margin related to supply and demand, and competitive factors between forfaiters.
7. The cost of the bank guarantee or aval, if applicable. This is linked to the relative credit rating of the buyer, as perceived by the guarantor bank.

The first six elements of cost are usually paid directly by the seller, and the seventh by the buyer. However, one way or another the total cost of forfaiting is part of the total cost of the goods supplied. In fact sellers often add their cost into the overall price. Therefore examining alternatives in respect of each component of the overall cost could enable you to offer a more competitive or more profitable package to your buyer – depending on the price sensitivity in the market.

5.15   SECURITIZATION

Securitization can only be considered a payment risk mitigant to the degree that it results in the transfer of payment risk to the related "special purpose vehicle" company (SPV) without recourse to your company, in both practice and theory.

Securitization SPVs are designed to meet the parameters required to obtain a certain investment rating from a rating agency. These parameters include stipulated maximum loss provisions. The rating determines the cost of the funds that must be attracted to finance the securitization programme. Therefore it is common practice for the entity that benefits from the programme to "remove" from the SPV any receivables that become delinquent or that default, and to replace them with sound receivables. In effect this means that the securitization programme is not a risk transfer mechanism. It is in reality only a means of raising lower-cost finance and/or of improving your apparent return on assets, by reducing the total value of the assets appearing on your corporation's balance sheet.

5.16   OTHER IDEAS AND CONCLUSION

Inevitably your company will uncover excellent commercial opportunities that are not creditworthy in the normal course, and that do not support the traditional forms of risk alleviation. Transactions of this ilk are the test of *real* credit professionals, demanding as they do the application of imagination, flexibility, knowledge, intense communication and close control. Not recommended for the faint-hearted and definitely not recommended if the exposure exceeds the amount your company can comfortably afford to lose, such transactions can nevertheless create meaningful competitive advantage if managed successfully.

Here are some ideas that could minimize the customer and/or country risk even in difficult cases.

5.16.1   Bonded (customs supervised) storage

Credit exposure can sometimes be minimized if goods can be delivered into bonded storage close to, or even at, the buyer's premises. If you can retain ownership until the buyer sells the goods and removes them from the bonded warehouse, receivable amounts will be minimized. The buyer will also often have the advantage of delaying payment of import duty and other taxes, accordingly conserving precious cash resources. This option is only available where local laws permit, such as in Croatia, for example.

5.16.2   Retention of ownership

Where local legislation permits, it may be possible for you to retain title in goods supplied and subsequently title in the resulting receivables, and in any cash realized. This effectively secures the credit against the goods at all times until payment is received.

5.16.3 Selling direct to better buyers

In cases where you supply a local distributor, you may be able to agree to contract a large delivery directly with the distributor's customer, in return for paying the distributor a service fee equivalent to its usual margin. In this way you could obtain a better quality receivable on your own books, and help to develop your distributor's business capacity.

5.16.4 Countertrade

In extremely difficult cases (or situations where your counterparty lacks the ability to monetize its goods) it may be possible to safely secure your receivable by taking goods supplied by your counterparty as a substitute for cash payment. In its least sophisticated form countertrade consists of pure barter, the exchange of one type of good for another.

Other alternatives include:

(a) Separate purchase and sale transactions with the cash from one used to offset the payment of the other, through an independently managed trust (escrow) account.
(b) Buy-back deals by means of which a supply of, say, machinery is later paid for by the buyer providing the seller with the related produce over an agreed period of time.
(c) Counter-purchase deals designed to bind a seller to buy a certain quantity of goods produced by the buyer and to dispose of them in markets not yet developed by the buyer.

Naturally as a seller contemplating a countertrade transaction, you would prefer to receive an internationally traded commodity. In other words, a commodity that has its price determined in a transparent and liquid market, that provides price risk hedging possibilities. Unfortunately few potential buyers will offer this type of good in exchange, therefore countertrade opportunities must be carefully examined and an additional "margin" must be incorporated in order to cover unforeseen difficulties. Countertrade challenges could include the obligation to purchase large quantities of goods that prove to be unmarketable, either due to quality issues or surplus supply, or the costs of transportation and marketing may be significantly underestimated.

On the positive side, if your organization is sufficiently diverse, your company may be able to extract more value from the goods bought in compensation than the seller perceives them to be worth. In other words, you could achieve an increase in overall margin by taking goods instead of cash, by way of settlement of a receivable. As mentioned above, the application of imagination, flexibility, knowledge, intense communication and close control can achieve exceptional results even in countertrade.

Thought for the day

Payment security will not save you from a dishonest buyer, so never omit your *due diligence* investigation.

Part II
Global Credit Power in the Twenty-first Century: The New Sources of Power

6

Receivable Asset Management – Portfolio Power

6.1 BACKGROUND

It is estimated that accounts receivable (trade debtors) amount to 28% of company assets, on average. This represents an enormous investment in working capital.

Most executives expect corporate assets to "work for their keep", to add value net of related costs, whether those assets are factory buildings, machines, fleets of vans, teams of employees, or offices. However, the accounts receivable portfolio is seldom considered a discrete asset so little attempt is made to extract its maximum value contribution. Granting credit can either be seen as an action involving "the provision of goods and/or services sometime before expecting payment" (lending a neighbour a cup of sugar), or it can be seen as "financing your customer's purchase of goods and services from you" (lending your neighbour 25c to buy a cup of sugar from you).

The attitude towards trade credit in the commercial field is often, "we manufacture and sell goods, therefore we grant credit, hence we have receivables, we should collect those receivables as quickly as possible, end of story". The tendency is to overlook the fact that – in the context of an ongoing business – each invoice collected is replaced by a fresh invoice, resulting in a body of cash being locked up (invested) indefinitely.

In the context of banking, the stock-in-trade is "money" and the supply of money is the core activity. Consequently there is no ambivalence towards receivables in banking circles. While bankers naturally expect customers to pay interest for money borrowed, they have also developed sophisticated techniques and instruments to enable them to maximize the value added by their loan portfolios (receivables). These techniques include securitization and credit derivatives.

Like it or not, choose it or not, by default or by dint of strategic decision, it is commercial undertakings that are the largest providers of short-term "venture" capital (working capital) in the form of supplier credit. Ironically it is not banks, nor is it venture capital funds that provide the bulk of working capital, rather it is suppliers that are the true venture capital providers, no matter how much they wish to avoid undertaking what is perceived as a banking role. Yet this function is usually not considered a core activity in companies, and is therefore not resourced as a core competency. Lacking resources and visibility at executive committee or Board level, credit risk administration is seldom in a position to reap the rewards of receivables portfolio management.

The new role for the commercial credit manager should be at the heart of the business, managing the receivable portfolio and establishing credit policy.

Most day-to-day, transaction-by-transaction credit management activities carried out today are already being successfully "outsourced" (contracted out to be provided by specialized businesses – see Chapter 8) by leading companies in virtually every field.

Credit executives will soon be recognized as having an important contribution to make as the strategic managers of the significant *investment* in accounts receivable, and of the risk profile of that investment.

Standard & Poor's (S&P) has announced that it will focus on the *concentration* and *correlation* risks of a company's counterparty portfolio (meaning its "receivable portfolio risks") when reviewing ratings, or when rating companies for the first time. The inference is that the overall quality of your company's receivable portfolio and measures taken to mitigate related risks will be taken into account when it is rated either formally (by one of the rating agencies) or informally, by banks or investors using processes that mimic rating agency methods. A company's credit rating directly impacts its cost of capital.

Receivables portfolio management tools are available, and others will be invented, to enable credit executives to manage the cost of capital, while providing improved transaction-by-transaction competitive advantage.

6.1.1   Cost of capital

The cost of capital is the average cost of borrowed funds (bank loans, for example) and equity. In practice it is a function of lenders' and investors' perceptions of the risk inherent in a business.

In the case of any company that owns and operates a significant investment in receivables, it follows that:

● The higher the receivable portfolio risk, the higher the company risk profile
● The higher the company risk profile, the higher the cost of capital

A higher cost of capital necessarily leads to lower total shareholder return; explicitly it leads to poorer performance. Thus the quality of the management of a receivables portfolio has a direct impact on overall corporate performance.

Obviously the quality of the management of credit risk in relation to individual transactions also impacts corporate performance on a cumulative basis, through its impact on gross turnover figures and bad debts written off. However, the micro-management of customer accounts is generally well understood. Conversely, the strategic management of receivables as a unitary asset is not common.

It is important to keep in mind the concept of *investment management* when considering the overall management and protection of receivables. It terms of this concept receivables should be managed at a macro-level using a portfolio approach, as well as at a micro-level.

The micro-management of receivables involves assessing individual banks, assessing individual customers and controlling individual deliveries. Macro-management is another *simultaneous* operation whereby the whole receivable portfolio is assessed and controlled with reference to its proportional composition on a credit rating class basis, on a country by country basis, and on an industry sector by industry sector basis.

A portfolio should also be analysed by industry or market segment, but since most companies operate in fairly narrow market segments (the segments for which they manufacture products or provide services) the related concentration risk is obvious, without the need for analysis.

The philosophy underlying portfolio management is the spreading of risks over various categories and over various layers, and the reduction of correlations and concentrations. This has the objective of ensuring that your company cannot be destroyed should one class of customer, or one sector, or one country, or one market segment fail.

Macro receivables management entails the notional sharing out of a portion or a multiple of your company's equity (own shareholders' funds) to each sector and country. This is done on the basis of the perceived risk of failure in each case, translated into an overall risk limit for each sector and country. The total exposure by credit rating class, by sector and by country should be monitored daily. If your company's exposure exceeds a segment limit at a particular time, the excess exposure has to be transferred to another segment.

Thus, for example, if the risk exposure in respect of country A exceeds the company's country A limit, the excess must be shifted to country B. This could perhaps be achieved by arranging for a bank in country B to guarantee a payment due from a buyer in country A. This action must be taken even if the buyer in question is a first-class credit risk. The buyer's status is not at issue in this example. The point at issue is the aggregate amount of exposure to country A. Since the country exposure exceeds the approved limit it must be reduced in order to keep the portfolio of risks in balance, protect the company and protect the company's own credit rating.

6.2   WHAT DOES ALL OF THIS MEAN TO ME, BOSS?

Credit Executive (CEx): I really appreciate the promotion, Boss, but this job description has me puzzled.

    Manage the receivables portfolio.
    Establish and maintain credit policy.
    Manage outsourced credit service providers.

I'm a multi-skilled professional with years of experience successfully managing counterparty payment risk, one-on-one, toe-to-toe, eye-to-eye, lunch-for-lunch. Is all my experience, legal training, accounting and analytical skill, and negotiation technique now redundant?

Chief Financial Officer (CFO): Well "yes" and "no". Your training, skills and experience are no longer needed in relation to individual orders or transactions or indeed customers. However, they will very definitely be needed in relation to the establishment of credit policies, policing those directives and fine-tuning them in future. Those activities will be a crucial part of your responsibility to see that our credit service providers perform effectively, and meet their agreed objectives.

CEx: (Thoughtfully) Oh, good, and what about this new number one priority, "manage the receivables portfolio"?

CFO: You've read the background note I provided, haven't you?

CEx: Yes. It's a bit theoretical though, "long" on philosophy and "short" on what I'm actually supposed to do.

CFO: Well it seems pretty straightforward to me. We have a receivables asset of about $500 million and you have the responsibility to make that asset work for the company – add value – rather than detract value. Granted it's not a refinery, nor a bread factory, in fact I'm not sure what it is (in detail) since we've never analysed the amorphous mass beyond ageing the invoices and working out the DSO [days sales outstanding]. Nevertheless you have contacts in the credit field, and in banking, you read the "trade press", you'll figure out what's needed. Work on it and let me know how you plan to achieve your goals in a week. Remember your most important goal is to avoid counter-party risk negatively affecting our credit rating. (Picking up telephone and punching several numbers) Oh, and to support sales growth, while reducing costs.

Sensing he had been dismissed, CEx grunted an acknowledgement and took himself out for coffee.

CEx spent a good deal of the following week researching receivable portfolio management and finally produced the following report.

MEMORANDUM TO CFO

MANAGING THE RECEIVABLES PORTFOLIO – A PROPOSAL

Dear CF

After our discussion last week, I analysed our receivables as they stood at the end of the last quarter. I looked at the overall agglomeration from five angles, namely:

- Exposure by industry sector.
- Exposure by country (actually I summed exposures in seven regions but separated out China).
- Exposure by credit rating class (using the familiar S&P scale).
- Exposure from the point of view of "concentration risk".
- Degrees of correlation between the various categories of exposure.

Please refer to the attached chart (Figure 6.1) to see a visualization of the portfolio exposure analysed by sector, country, and credit rating respectively.

The chart provides an easy to grasp picture of the more important facets of our receivables portfolio and how those components relate to each other. It should be a relatively simple matter to superimpose credit limits so that exposure excesses become immediately apparent, on a daily basis.

Had we not been operating an internal credit rating system for a couple of years now I would have had to invent one, in order to rate the some 80% of our customers that do not have public corporate credit ratings. Likewise our existing categorizations of counterparty exposures by country and industry sector were indispensable, as I'm sure you can imagine.

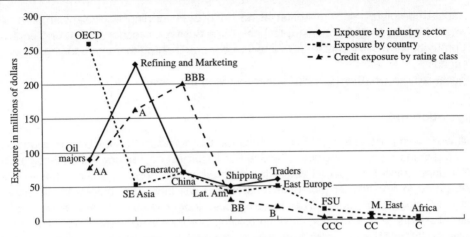

Figure 6.1   Accounts receivable portfolio risk analysis illustration

In terms of *concentration risk*, all of our exposure is focused in the energy and chemical raw materials market segments because of the very nature of our business. We find and extract crude oil so we have to either sell it to refiners, or refine it ourselves and sell it to wholesalers or consumers of refined petroleum products.

Most businesses are in the same position regarding concentration risk, especially since it has been fashionable to break up large diversified conglomerates in recent years. This has led to polarization in industry and commerce, with each company focusing on its core competencies. Consolidation trends in many market segments have worsened this situation, by reducing the number of buyers for many products and services.

However, do not be afraid of concentration risk for I know of an ingenious "cost free" solution.

Recommendations

- I will recommend country and industry sector limits. I will also recommend a maximum weighted average default probability objective for our portfolio. These recommendations will only be formulated after consulting with all interested parties internally, and our rating agency.
- I will arrange for a portfolio risk analysis chart to be produced daily, as per the illustration presented in Figure 6.1.
- I propose to monitor the respective exposures against the limits daily, and to take action to mitigate any excess exposures promptly.

Concentration risk mitigation

Concentration risk can be reduced to acceptable proportions by executing a bilateral payment risk swap contract with a suitable corporation. The latter will

(a) have to carry an equivalent credit rating to ours, and
(b) have a receivables portfolio that consists of customers operating in a market segment that is countercyclical to ours.

We could complete this transaction at no cost, by swapping equivalent amounts of payment (delinquency and bankruptcy) risk, thus buying protection and selling equivalent protection. This will enable us to improve our credit rating thereby reducing our cost of capital.

Please advise whether I should further research this idea.

Correlation risk

I will work with consultants to create scenarios that forecast the outcome of a one- or two-step credit rating downgrade affecting our 10 largest customers. This will help us to better understand correlations within the receivables portfolio. It is likely that smaller participants in our market (our other customers) will face downgrades if our largest customers are downgraded. That in turn could trigger collateral calls, setting off a chain of events potentially negatively impacting our own credit rating. My intention is to use the information gathered from this exercise to develop correlation risk mitigation strategies. Correlation risk is closely related to concentration risk so the solution may well lie in the utilization of a bilateral swap, as already described.

Portfolio weighted average default probability opportunity

I will be in a position to support marketing, when we have agreed the maximum weighted average default probability target for our receivables portfolio. I will then be able to shift the average down at a reasonable cost, and simultaneously accept some more risky counterparties, thus supporting sales growth without increasing the overall risk profile of our portfolio. Please refer to the following charts (Figures 6.2 and 6.3) to see an illustration of how this proposal could work in practice.

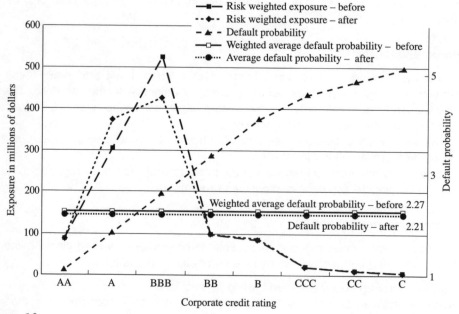

Figure 6.2

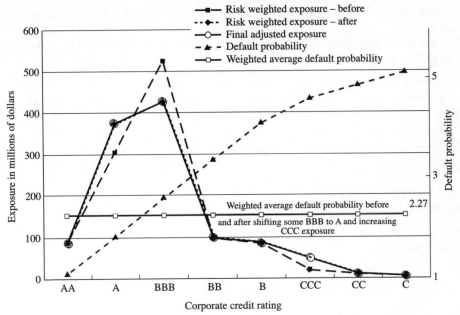

Figure 6.3

The first chart (Figure 6.2) initially illustrates the weighted average exposure of our current portfolio, based on estimated default probabilities across the corporate credit rating categories. The second exposure curve shows the effect of upgrading some receivables rated BBB to rating A by, for example, obtaining the payment guarantee of an A rated bank. The result of this category transfer is reflected in a reduction of the weighted average default probability from 2.27 to 2.21, in this example.

The second chart (Figure 6.3) illustrates that subsequently increasing our exposure to CCC rated counterparties can be accomplished without exceeding the original weighted average default probability of 2.27.

The cost of "upgrading" a BBB risk to an A risk should be lower than the cost of purchasing payment risk protection for a CCC risk, if the latter is available at all.

I look forward to discussing these recommendations in due course.

Regards CE

6.3   MANAGING THE PORTFOLIO DYNAMIC OF TRANSACTIONS

In order to effectively manage your company's receivables portfolio, processes must be in place to ensure that individual transactions (sales contracts) facilitate portfolio operations. This may mean, for instance, that you will require every buyer to issue a payment undertaking, to enable the acquisition of payment risk cover in the form of a risk-sharing agreement should this become desirable (see Chapter 13). The following example scenario illustrates the need to build such a degree of flexibility into every sales contract.

Assume that your company's capital (own shareholders' funds) equals $50 million, and in this example your company has the following approved credit limits:

A rated countries: 10 times own funds (i.e. $500 million per "A" rated country)
C rated countries: 0.6 times own funds (i.e. $30 million per "C" rated country)
A rated sectors: 5 times own funds (i.e. $250 million per "A" rated sector)
D rated sectors: 0.4 times own funds (i.e. $20 million per "D" rated sector)
Banks: 7 times own funds (i.e. $350 million)

yielding limits of:

Switzerland $500 million
Hungary $30 million

Refineries $250 million
Traders $20 million
Banks $350 million

Your company also has the following customer credit limits in place:

Refinery A Hungary $10 million
Refinery B Hungary $5 million
Refinery C Hungary $25 million

Trader A Hungary $1 million
Trader B Switzerland $20 million

Bank A Hungary $5 million
Bank B Switzerland $50 million

6.3.1 A scenario for illustration purposes

In all cases payment terms are "payment in full 30 days after the date of delivery or the date of the bill of lading". Figure 6.4 expresses the following scenario graphically:

- *Day One*: Refinery A in Hungary owes your company $15 million for a crude oil delivery. Your company obtains a $5 million payment guarantee from Bank A in Hungary to cover the excess over Refinery A's credit limit.
- *Day Two*: Refinery B in Hungary purchases a crude oil cargo worth $20 million and provides an LC, opened by Bank A in Hungary, to cover the full amount. Your company arranges for Bank B in Switzerland to confirm this Letter of Credit, thus covering the excess risk in the name of Bank A, and converting this exposure from Hungarian to Swiss country risk.
- *Day Three*: Refinery C in Hungary agrees to take delivery of two cargoes of crude oil worth a total of $25 million. This is acceptable in terms of the customer credit risk limit but, when added to the exposure to Refinery A ($10 million net) and Bank A ($5 million net), it causes the Hungarian country limit to be exceeded.

Your company decides to ask Bank B in Switzerland to provide silent (not disclosed to Refinery C) payment risk cover for $10 million of your company's

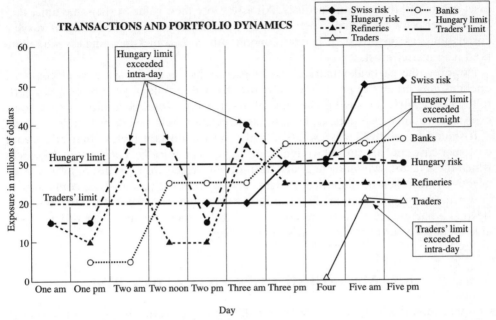

Figure 6.4 Transactions and portfolio dynamics

exposure to Refinery C. This converts $10 million of that exposure from Hungarian refinery risk to Swiss bank risk.

- *Day Four*: Trader A Hungary agrees a "contract for differences" with a mark-to-market[1] exposure of $1 million. This contract is established on open account (unsecured) terms.
- *Day Five*: Trader B in Switzerland purchases a cargo of crude oil worth $20 million. At the micro-level this is acceptable on open account but it causes the "Trader" sector limit to be exceeded. Therefore your company takes action to convert the $1 million of exposure with Trader A to bank risk, by obtaining silent payment risk cover from Bank B in Switzerland. This simultaneously takes care of the existing Hungary country limit exposure excess.

6.4 MANAGING CORRELATION RISK

The interrelationships between and among the various facets of a receivables portfolio are in themselves complex. Varying degrees of correlation add another layer of complexity.

Obtaining the precise correlation coefficients necessary to build a computer model of your receivables portfolio is not likely to be cost justified. It has anyway been found that correlations change as market conditions change. In fact correlations tend to approach one as market conditions deteriorate. Intuitively when markets collapse all

---

[1] "Mark-to-market" means "evaluated in comparison with a ruling market price on a particular day or at a particular time".

asset values will drop simultaneously. All assets lose their value at the same time, they become perfectly correlated. Therefore any careful analysis and modelling of varying correlations, as they exist in better economic times, becomes meaningless when you need it to matter most.

However, the particular market and/or geographic region in which your company operates may present opportunities to reduce the risk profile of your receivables portfolio. Deliberately managing the mix of risks within your portfolio so that some exposures counteract others, at least to some extent, could be a worthwhile strategy.

It should be relatively easy to identify the most important factors that affect your customer base, and are subject to significant change periodically. The varying degrees to which these factors will influence each facet of your receivables portfolio, positively or negatively, can then be discerned. Insights gained from such an analysis could lead to powerful decisions being made regarding sector and country limits, for instance. Beyond a narrow focus on the receivables portfolio, such insights could provide valuable input for your company's marketing strategy.

6.5   MANAGING CONCENTRATION RISK

Concentration risk is simply correlation risk by another name, but it is convenient to address two aspects separately under this heading. The first aspect is the probability, if not inevitability, that all of your receivable exposure will be concentrated in one market or industry segment – the segment in which you operate and/or in which your company excels by deploying its core competencies. If this is the case, recognition of the concentration risk could lead to the creation of a plan to broaden the range of customers for your product or service, thus positively influencing the growth and future stability of your company.

The second feature of concentration relates to the risks inherent when a relatively large proportion of a company's receivables portfolio is owed by relatively few customers. The danger of default of one customer is much greater than the danger of default of several occurring at the same time. Hence if single customers each account for a large proportion of receivables, the risks posed by such concentration are apparent.

In this respect, again, the realization of this situation could lead to the adoption of activities designed to minimize the threat posed to the survival of the company. Unfortunately the policy and strategic changes that a company can make to limit concentration risk often require an extended period of time to be fully implemented and only partially achieve the objective.

A parallel or substitute approach to reducing concentration risk is available. It involves the use of one or more payment risk swaps.

6.5.1   Payment risk swaps

A payment risk swap provides your company with the ability to reduce its exposure to credit risk in respect of some of its customers, without impacting its business relationship with those customers in any way. This can be achieved using *credit derivatives*, but at the cost of the related premiums and with the acquisition of new risks. The main inhibitor to the use of credit derivatives is "basis risk", that is, the lack of correlation between the changes exhibited by the "reference asset" of a credit derivative and the changes exhibited at the same time by the receivable asset you are trying to cover. In addition the "specified credit events" that would trigger a credit derivative do not always match the delinquency (late payment) or default (failure to pay) events specific to your trade receivable. Moreover, to the extent that your customers do not issue any publicly traded debt instruments, the only way to utilize this mechanism to mitigate concentration risk is to choose an unrelated "reference asset". This would amplify the basis risks described; see section 5.10 for details.

In summary, the use of credit derivatives could reduce concentration risk, but will cost money and will add new risks to your portfolio.

6.5.2   Bilateral swap contracts

An alternative practice would involve your company in seeking out another company with a similar need but a completely different receivables portfolio. It may be possible to reduce concentration risk by executing a bilateral payment risk swap contract with such a firm. The swap would only be effective if your counterparty had (a) an equivalent credit rating to yours, and (b) a receivables portfolio that consisted of customers operating in a market segment that was countercyclical to yours.

Subject to receipt of supportive legal and tax advice, having found a creditworthy counterparty with a similar need but different portfolio, you could agree a bilateral swap on the basis of no cost to either party. In terms of such an agreement, each party would consent to compensate the other should the other suffer any "loss given default" (LGD) in respect of specified customers, up to agreed maximum amounts.

As a result each party would effectively replace payment risk in respect of a subset (or portion of a subset) of its own customers with the similarly rated payment risk of some customers of the other, from a completely different market segment or industry. Each party's relationship with its own customers would not be affected in any way, but its own receivables portfolio risk profile would be improved by means of a reduction in concentration risk. This is an elegant solution. The only challenge is finding an ideal counterparty.

7

Electronic Commerce – Internet Power

7.1 INTRODUCTION

Internet technology and accessibility have changed the nature of work in many occupations. Change is advancing on all fronts, not least in respect of credit and receivables management. The change referred to is not the sort of ripple experienced in the past, it is a seismic wave of inconceivable power and implications. It is the fabled "third wave" and as Canute the Great may have said when the tide washed in over his feet, "Let all know how empty and worthless is the power of a credit manager, for there is none able to prevent the tsunami of change from sweeping away the dearly loved status quo."

The sandcastles of status-quo-credit-management-methodology carefully crafted day by day will soon be swept away, despite all protestations that "it has always been done this way" or "this is the only way to do the job".

"The networked economy (is) besieging the old world with the most sophisticated weaponry ever seen" (Carayol and Firth, 2001: 1). In the words of Professor Richard Scase, the third wave is a tidal wave

> creating a new culture of how we do business; a new culture which is based *on an anti-business business approach*, a culture of business which is very much twenty-first century, unlike the culture of management which we have today, which is often nineteenth century for many businesses . . . technology is creating a far greater need to leverage human capital more effectively than in the past. (Scase, 2000)

New technology has been and is being developed, and is available to everyone, everywhere, all of the time, through the internet. The implications are difficult to grasp, and impossible to turn to advantage unless processes, organization structures, and attitudes change to allow internet power to work its magic.

"In our enterprises today, the search for talent is everything. It is all about recruiting, orienting, socializing, retaining, and renewing commitment and the social contract between employer and employee" (Henschel, 2001). Unlocking the power of the internet is not about youth versus experience, it is about vision, it is about a willingness to let go of the past, and a willingness to embrace the new opportunities presented. It is about attitude and about courage. It is about talented people operating in a corporate environment conducive to change.

"The quicker you let go of old cheese, the sooner you find new cheese" (Johnson, 1998: 60). Intellectually it is relatively easy to make a case for embracing some or all of the opportunities offered through the internet, on grounds of "return on investment" and/or efficiency and/or competitive advantage. Still the take-up rates for these offerings is relatively low, even disappointing.

In many organizations "credit" is still seen as a necessary evil, rather than a key part of the product mix, with potential to increase stockholder (shareholder) value. In this light it is difficult to persuade senior executives to divert investment resources to enable the successful implementation of new technology. Credit employees are left to focus on collections without any hope of rather improving the order-to-cash process[1] and minimizing collections, while ringing in their ears are constant admonitions to "do more with less people".

Other firms have credit personnel who do all they can to preserve the status quo because that means they can carry on doing the things they love doing, the things they do well, the things that earned them promotions in the past. These duties include "financial analysis" and "conjuring up credit limit decisions based on intuition, art and not much science". People with this attitude will argue that there is "no other way", that important "relationships will be lost", and that what they do has "always worked" so should not be changed.

In some cases, however, the new product or process offered has just been too revolutionary for many to envision. The step away from the present into the future has just been too bold, too radical. The product offer of Bolero.net is a good example of this providing, as it does, for the dematerialization of paper documents. Businesses can move from "paper trade documents" to "no paper at all" almost overnight. However, for many this is a "giant leap" when "small steps" would be preferred.

A typical international credit risk management department incurs expenses in the proportions shown in this table:

Processing LCs	48%
Monitoring and collecting receivables	20%
Credit research and analysis	25%
Finding and negotiating credit risk cover	7%

Automating the order-to-cash process, using electronic document management technology (including XML, extensible markup language), and using the internet as the communications medium, could considerably reduce the cost of both "processing LCs" and "monitoring and collecting" receivables. "Credit research and analysis" is the other major component of credit management costs that could be positively impacted utilizing web technology.

The only caveat is that a credit department is unlikely to realize the maximum efficiencies if it is acting alone. Cross-function change will be necessary, particularly across the whole order-to-cash process, sometimes called the financial value chain (FVC).

Internet-based technology can improve your company's total shareholder return in four respects; automation of the order-to-cash process (including credit risk mitigation instruments), providing new credit risk mitigation techniques, credit analysis and decision, and finding credit risk cover efficiently.

---

[1] Order-to-cash process – this describes the entire sales process from taking the customer's order, to checking the customer's credit status, to establishing a line of credit or requesting an LC, to completing the sell/buy contract, to placing the order, to checking inventory and picking the order, to examining and accepting the LC if required, to releasing any credit hold, to shipping the product, to invoicing, to presenting documents to the LC bank if required, to receiving the payment, to marking the invoice as paid.

7.2   AUTOMATION OF THE ORDER-TO-CASH PROCESS

Several internet-based (web-based) systems are available to enable the automation of the order-to-cash process involving international or domestic trade, including the use of documents of title (ownership) such as bills of lading. These include systems provided by:

- Bolero.net SURF (Settlement Utility for Risk and Finance) (http://www. bolero.net)
- @GlobalTrade (http://www.globaltradecorp.com)
- Standard Chartered Bank's B2BeX (http://www.scb2bex.com)
- JPMorgan's Trade Information Exchange (TIE) (http://ts.jpmorgan.com)

The benefits that can be captured using straight through processing (STP)[2] or, to a lesser extent, a mixture of electronic documents and traditional paper incorporate:

- No rekeying of data
- No telex or fax costs
- No courier costs
- Less delay
- No garbled messages
- No letters of indemnity for missing documents (LoIs)
- No gathering, checking and packaging of paper documents
- Fewer LC amendments
- No advising banks
- Earlier credit hold releases
- No people checking documents, payments and receipts
- No document discrepancies, against LC requirements
- No manual message authentication (test key) arrangements
- No payment delays
- No inflated credit exposures, due to delays in marking invoices paid

It has been estimated that savings of at least $500 per export transaction could be realized, but the exporter in a chain is not the only beneficiary. All parties involved in the transaction process will be able to "bank" cost savings.

7.2.1   An example sales transaction with LC and STP

This example describes a fictional ideal process that is nevertheless feasible in terms of available technology, legal and security considerations.

An order is taken, or sell/buy deal agreed, including credit terms of "LC required" (after consultation with the relevant database or credit officer).

The details of the specific deal are entered into an electronic "deal entry form".

The system uses the deal entry data to populate a contract template, generating a contract automatically. The contracts administrator reviews the contract on screen and, if satisfied, "posts" or "uploads" it onto a secure website. The system then sends an

---

[2] STP refers to a process that requires basic data related to each transaction to be entered only once, then reused to populate other documents through to the end of the process chain.

email to the buyer requesting review and approval of the contract. There is no rekeying of data from the deal entry and there are no telex or fax costs incurred.

The buyer opens the secure website and reviews the contract, makes a note of suggested amendments – if any – and initiates an email message to the seller requesting a review of the amendments. An "off-line" negotiation phase ensues – probably via telephone – to agree final contract terms.

The seller then posts the final contract details on the secure website and the buyer accepts the contract. A contract is then available, with the essential data related to the transaction in XML format, accessible to authorized parties via a standard web browser. Time will be saved in this contract finalization phase, telex and fax costs will be avoided, and STP will be enabled.

The seller's shipping department will receive an email instruction to view the contract on the secure website. It will proceed to create the packing list, inspection requests, and shipping instructions by transferring data from the contract into relevant templates. Saving the templates will generate email messages addressed to the warehouse and third-party service providers (inspectors and freight forwarders). There is no rekeying of data (less opportunity for errors to occur) and communication costs are reduced.

Simultaneously the buyer accesses the secure website and uses the contract data to populate an LC issuance request addressed to its bank. This is saved and a message is sent to the credit officer of the seller requesting a review of the request. When the request text is agreed it is saved on the website and an email is sent to the bank asking it to review and act upon the request.

The bank opens the LC advising it by SWIFT message to the seller's appointed bank. The latter uploads the SWIFT message to the secure website and the seller's credit officer ensures it conforms to the seller's requirements.

The seller's credit officer then releases the "credit hold" on the cargo.

The warehouse, freight forwarder and inspector then produce the final packing list, bill of lading and inspection certificate respectively, using templates and the data on the secure website. No rekeying of data reduces errors and speeds up the process. In addition the documents are all immediately available on the secure website, either for printing at a bank or for further processing electronically (depending on the level of sophistication reached). No rekeying errors, no transmission delays, and no courier costs result.

The seller's accounting department then finalize the invoice template on the secure website. The invoice is already partially completed with XML data lifted from the contract, the shipping documents, and the LC. No rekeying errors and less delay.

The credit officer reviews the invoice and shipping documents on the secure website and initiates a message to the processing bank, requesting the bank to review, accept and pay against the documents. No courier, telex or fax costs, and no delay.

The bank either manually or automatically (depending on the level of sophistication reached) reviews the documents and initiates the payment to the seller. The XML content of the documents presented enables the bank to achieve savings based on automatic document checking. eUCP[3] rules enable banks to accept presentations under LCs consisting of electronic documents only, or a combination of electronic

---

[3] eUCP – Supplement to UCP 500 for electronic presentation, Version 1.0. UCP 500 – International Chamber of Commerce (ICC) Uniform Customs and Practice for Documentary Credits (ICC Publication number 500).

and paper documents. No need to issue a letter of indemnity for missing documents (LoI), no telex, fax or courier charges (if presentation is purely electronic), no document discrepancies, no delays or documentary risks[4] in obtaining payment.

The processing bank then arranges reimbursement of amounts it has paid to the seller, and releases the documents to the buyer. This reduces the likelihood that the buyer will have to issue an LoI in order to obtain the goods, or ensures that any LoI issued can be promptly redeemed.

The paying bank sends an electronic payment advice to the seller referencing the seller's invoice, based on the XML data embedded in that invoice. The seller's treasury department feeds this advice into the accounting system, the invoice is automatically matched and marked paid. If the system cannot match the payment with the invoice it produces an exception or "repair" report for the immediate attention of the accountant. Invoices are automatically marked as paid and credit exposures automatically reduced.

7.3 NEW CREDIT RISK MITIGATION TECHNIQUES

TradeCard (http://www.tradecard.com) provides a good example of a new credit risk mitigation process that harnesses the power of the internet, bringing to its users all of the benefits of STP already enumerated. TradeCard has been commercially available since the first quarter of 2000.

When potential buyers and sellers agree to utilize the TradeCard system, it allows them to negotiate the contract terms via the internet. Once a contract, in the form of a purchase order, is agreed the buyer and seller formally confirm the terms through TradeCard. The transaction has a payment guarantee attached so the seller is certain to be paid automatically upon compliance with the terms of the purchase order.

7.3.1 TradeCard prerequisites

- Both buyer and seller must register and receive passwords for at least two employees each.
- TradeCard uses 128 bit SSL security technology with "Verisign" signatures. Each signatory is issued with a smart card which generates a random number in a portable card reader.
- All buyers must be qualified by Coface,[5] either by means of the Coface @rating "@@@@" symbol via the website (http://www.cofacerating.com) or specially qualified, or qualified by GE Commercial Services (http://www.geccs.com).
- Buyers must also give an agreed authorized bank a mandate to electronically debit their bank account.
- Only standard internet browsers (Microsoft Internet Explorer, for example) are needed to access TradeCard.

[4] Documentary risk – the risk that a loss will be incurred because of errors in documents presented for payment under an LC.
[5] Coface (http://www.coface.com) is a credit insurance provider operating worldwide.

7.3.2 The TradeCard process

Figure 7.1 shows a process flow chart for a typical transaction utilizing TradeCard.

- The buyer completes a purchase order (PO) online, and the system sends an email to designated persons working for the seller.
- The seller opens a work list and reviews the PO. After negotiation – if necessary – the seller confirms the PO. Two levels of confirmation are required.
- After shipping the goods, the seller completes a partially pre-populated invoice and packing list on the website.
- The shipper (a third party that has been accepted by Coface in order to avoid fraud) posts an e-Waybill – or equivalent – on the website, and sends the paper original to the buyer as usual. The shipper "guarantees" that the e-Waybill represents a genuine document.
- The TradeCard patented compliance engine checks that the documents comply with the agreed PO. If there is non-compliance email messages alert buyer and seller. The parties then negotiate and accept the discrepancies, subject to whatever change in the terms is agreed. The "compliance engine" then sets to work again to confirm all is in compliance, based on the new parameters.
- Then the agreed authorized bank is set to work debiting the buyer's account, by means of an ACH debit or reverse MT202, and crediting the seller's account, upon receipt of cleared funds.

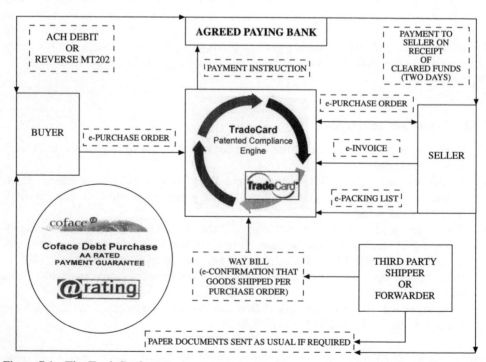

Figure 7.1 The TradeCard process

- If the buyer does not have funds, Coface pays the seller. Coface is AA rated by FitchRatings.
- This process does not involve UCP 500, nor does it involve any banks (except the authorized paying bank only in respect of the cash transaction).

The TradeCard process offers a potential win–win for some buyers and sellers if (a) the buyer's credit risk is accepted by either Coface or GE Commercial Services, and (b) the overall cost is cheaper than a traditional LC transaction.

Normally credit risks can be accepted on transactions where the individual amount of exposure is around $100 000 and charges are usually better than competitive. In addition every transaction is completely transparent and easy to track at every stage. These latter points provide corporate treasurers with much improved cash flow related information.

7.4   CREDIT ANALYSIS AND DECISION

It is aptly noted on the website of eCredit.com Inc. (http://www.ecredit.com) that:

> In a world moving at Internet speed, businesses require the ability to process credit and financing applications in seconds rather than days. Yet most credit decisions are still made through a manual process – a process that is slow, complicated and inconsistent.

Although eCredit.com has a vested interest in this statement proving to be true, since it markets a successful solution, the assertion is difficult to refute. The volume of business to business transactions concluded through internet websites is growing exponentially. With this growth comes the need for payment assurance. How can sellers ensure that they are paid for goods dispatched when the buyer is unknown and there is precious little time – perhaps seven seconds or so – to conduct an investigation?

Individuals have used credit cards to guarantee payment for web purchases, and the owners of small businesses have done likewise. Some companies have issued "purchase cards" (a form of corporate credit card) to employees to enable them to make small purchases either in the traditional manner (thus reducing the numbers of payables processed) or via the web. However, these solutions have limitations. The most serious of these is that they cannot cover larger acquisitions, so there is a danger that transactions will revert to traditional processes, after an initial introduction is effected over the internet.

There are two ways to deal with the credit question that threatens to derail the development of business to business via sellers' own websites, or via Vortals,[6] Portals,[7] e-Exchanges and e-Markets. The two options are "pre-qualification", and "instant decisions".

---

[6] Vortal – Vertical Industry Portal is a website that provides information and resources (including access to relevant goods and services suppliers) for a particular industry.
[7] Web Portal – a website that offers a broad range of resources and services, including online shopping. Most search engines, such as Yahoo!, have transformed themselves into Web Portals to attract and keep a larger clientele. A Web Portal is usually referred to simply as a "portal". Source: http://www.webopedia.com.

7.4.1 Authentication

However, before entertaining any transaction over the web a seller must establish the authenticity of the business applicant. Does the internet enquirer represent a genuine business, and is the enquirer authorized to contract a purchase on behalf of the business apparently represented?

There are several ways to establish authenticity; for example, Experian (http://www.experian.com) and D&B (http://www.dnb.com) provide products that enable the authentication of customers based on information they provide online. This may involve live interaction with the agency's database or verification of electronic client certificates, a form of digital identity card.

7.4.2 Pre-qualification

e-Exchange arrangements

In order to transact business in many e-Exchanges or e-Markets, particularly Vortals, it is necessary for companies to apply for membership and for all counterparties to decide whether to grant credit to them or not. The Intercontinental Exchange (ICE)[8] is a good example of this approach.

The ICE system allows each participant to decide with which counterparties it is prepared to trade, the maximum time period forward exposures can be agreed, and the maximum daily credit exposure limit allowed. The traders on behalf of each participant will only be allowed to consider executing deals that are posted on the system anonymously by "qualified" counterparties. That is, offers by counterparties that have been accepted, provided those offers are within the pre-set parameters of time and credit limit.

Intra-day (daily) ICE limits are not additional credit limits. They are used by the ICE system to establish which deals your traders will be able to choose to "trade". This is determined by the ICE system deducting the notional exposure of any deals concluded by your company with the counterparty "today" and the notional exposure of the deal represented by the (offer) price posted. If the total is within the intra-day limit, the price will be colour coded to indicate your trader can choose to trade that deal. Only after a deal has been concluded is the counterparty's identity revealed.

If a counterparty's notional exposure during any day reaches a predetermined "trigger" amount, a warning email will be sent to your nominated credit administrators. This will give them an opportunity to revise the intra-day limit, if that is appropriate.

Intra-day limits are all refreshed at the start of each trading day. That is to say, each day the full intra-day limit is available at the start of the day. Credit exposure management is undertaken on your internal system, not on ICE. Therefore it is vital that any trades concluded via ICE must be promptly entered into your internal system.

If an ICE counterparty exceeds its credit limit on your internal system and it is decided to call for any additional transactions to be fully secured, the related intra-day limit should be reduced to zero.

---

[8] Intercontinental Exchange (http://www.intcx.com), widely referred to as "ICE", enables the trading of over 600 commodities (physical and derivatives) in the precious metals, petroleum, natural gas and power sectors on a bilateral (over the counter) basis 24 hours a day worldwide. ICE is also the owner of the International Petroleum Exchange (IPE).

Third-party recommendation

This form of qualification for trade credit can either come from a third party that actually provides a concomitant payment guarantee, or one that merely offers to provide a payment guarantee on request. Alternatively it may simply be a neutral opinion in the form of a trade credit rating or score.

Credit score

In relatively few countries it is possible to purchase credit scores from agencies that have sufficient consistent data available to produce statistically reliable default predictors. The USA is the most developed marketplace in this respect, with proprietary credit risk scores available from various suppliers including D&B and Experian. In countries that do not have the necessary data available, credit scores simply cannot be obtained from third-party agencies.

Public credit rating

Relatively few companies, in the global context, have public credit ratings created by agencies like FitchRatings (http://www.fitchibca.com), Moody's (http://www.moodys.com) or S&P (http://www.sandp.com), since they have to commission these themselves at a relatively high cost. Companies have to reap considerable benefit from obtaining a public credit rating to justify the cost. Public credit ratings are associated with multi-million dollar bond issues or similar fund-raising activities in most cases.

Recommendation and optional guarantee

The service provided by Coface @rating (http://www.cofacerating.com) contrasts with other public rating offerings. Coface @rating provides both a public credit rating (of 41 million companies in 176 countries) and an offer to guarantee (credit insure) any exposure up to a rating related limit, provided the seller has an insurance policy with Coface. Coface @ratings apply up to a maximum credit of USD/EUR100 000.

A company that is not already rated by Coface @rating can request a rating. Coface @rating will charge a small fee and require certain minimum information, in order to rate a company. The company requesting an @rating may choose not to have the rating published, if it is not satisfied with the result.

7.4.3 Instant decisions

Automation of the credit decision-making process in the context of business to business web commerce has been successfully implemented by several companies. Some of these have formed alliances with certain banks to enable the provision of offers to finance purchases within nanoseconds, rather than weeks.

The decision support software provided by eCredit.com Inc. (http://www.ecredit.com) is a good example of what can be achieved. A customer's credit information is collected at the point of sale, then it is automatically processed using your credit policies, your scorecards, and data that you specify from your internal systems and from information providers (such as D&B and Experian). If bank financing is required the score and credit information can be forwarded to a panel of banks for computerized review. Panel banks' systems go through a similar process of review and return financing offers automatically. Most transactions are processed without human intervention, providing near-instant credit decisions while the customer is connected to your website.

7.5   FINDING CREDIT RISK COVER EFFICIENTLY

7.5.1   Trade finance and/or payment risk auction sites

LTPTrade (http://www.ltp.com) and ELCY Limited (http://www.elcy.com) provide auction sites for trade-related credit risk, with and without finance options respectively. Sellers can place details of transactions on a secure website, and invite a panel of banks to offer pricing to cover either bank credit risk (by confirming LCs) or corporate credit risk, using payment undertakings and risk-sharing agreements (see Chapter 13). This has created a more transparent and competitive market for trade-related payment risk. It has also reduced the time spent by corporate credit officers calling individual banks in order to elicit quotes, and negotiating transaction details. In combination these two benefits reduce costs significantly. An important additional benefit is the ability to prove to sales or trading colleagues that the best deal available was obtained.

Traditional trade finance bankers lament the effect this type of development will have on "relationships", but banks find they also benefit. They are offered more transactions, and the market price level for various risks is easier to establish. In the latter respect auction sites are able to add value by providing aggregated anonymous market information.

8

Outsourcing – Alliance Power

8.1 INTRODUCTION

Outsourcing is no longer simply an employee-number-reducing or cost-cutting exercise. It is a strategic decision that, properly executed, turns non-core yet critical activities into vibrant value-adding ventures.

Many companies already undertake tactical outsourcing when particular tasks require the injection of temporary extra resources. This may involve hiring a specialized team to bring annual account reviews up to date, for example. A firm stipulates its requirements and the service is provided accordingly. When the task is complete the contract ends.

Additionally a plethora of outsource providers has developed to service one or other part of the credit function, such as collections, deduction management and dispute resolution. This has been a response to the way in which credit activities have traditionally been organized within companies. The existence of discrete teams dealing with various credit-related activities has bred service providers specializing in those same tasks. These service providers take advantage of economies of scale, the pooling of expertise and the use of technologies that individual companies cannot support on their own. The most prominent examples of this type of service are "collection" and "deduction or dispute resolution" services, services providing for the perfection of collateral, such as a security interest or charge over movable assets, for example inventory or equipment, credit investigation services, credit risk analysis and cash applications.

8.2 IMPLICATIONS FOR TRADE CREDIT MANAGEMENT

Outsourcing is not a preferred solution for all situations involving trade credit management. Generally there are three aspects to an outsourcing decision:

1. *Economy of scale*. Outsource if the decision will capture economies of scale.
2. *Credit expertise*. If you do not have the necessary expertise to manage the credit function optimally within your company, outsource with a partner that does.
3. *Degree of risk*. A receivables portfolio that contains a high degree of risk, particularly customer concentration risk (few high exposure customers), indicates against a decision to outsource, unless it is possible to take some action that will significantly reduce the degree of risk at the portfolio level.

Therefore if an "outsourcing partner" is able to offer economies of scale and access to credit expertise your company does not possess, and your portfolio is considered "low risk" (small amounts owed by many customers or comprised of a highly creditworthy customer base), then a decision to outsource will be supported by the "three tests".

It is feasible for many companies to outsource most of the activities traditionally associated with in-house trade or commercial credit management. Commercial credit activities that can be outsourced include:[1]

Collections	Billing/invoicing
Credit analysis	Credit scoring
Management reporting	Customer service
Accounts receivable	Global risk management
Legal/bankruptcy	Inventory control
Cash applications	Cash forecasting
Customer visits	Cash flow management
Supplier analysis	

This leaves credit managers with five main areas of activity, namely:

- Developing credit policy
- Setting credit terms
- Managing trade finance bank relationships
- Managing receivables service providers
- Working capital management

Outsourcing to this extent brings a different emphasis to the job, shifting the focus from "the micro-management of individual receivables" to "the macro-management of the receivables portfolio".

8.3   OUTSOURCING ORDER-TO-CASH

Credit management functions – although often managed in a separate unit – are in fact an integral part of the order-to-cash process[2] of most companies. An "outsourcing partner" or "managed services provider" with a well-structured mandate can integrate the whole process, even across the boundaries of entrenched functional silos. Outsourcing adds to this the transformation in employees' attitudes that accompanies a move from working in a "cost creating support role" to providing "value adding services" in an enterprise that seeks to maximize its share of savings generated, while improving the customer experience provided. The results achieved through this approach have been significant. One "managed services provider" that works with Global 1000 companies has reported that it has reduced working capital requirements

---

[1] Lists from *The Credit and Financial Management Review* (1997: 16). A report created by the Credit Research Foundation (http://www.crfonline.org) based on extensive focus groups and a survey conducted in the USA, during 1996/97.
[2] Order-to-cash process – this describes the entire sales process from taking the customer's order, to checking the customer's credit status, to establishing a line of credit or requesting an LC, to completing the sell/buy contract, to placing the order, to checking inventory and picking the order, to examining and accepting the LC if required, to releasing any credit hold, to shipping the product, to invoicing, to presenting documents to the LC bank or resolving any dispute, to receiving the payment, to marking the invoice as paid, analysing and reporting.

over three companies by $800 million, resulting in interest savings of some $48 million per annum. At the same time it recorded improvements in customer satisfaction levels (French and Gai, 2003).

It is feasible to gain some of these advantages by outsourcing parts of the credit management process. However, since customers do not see the order-to-cash process in terms of a series of disconnected departments, executives should question why they are organized in that way. Fragmenting the order-to-cash process and subsequently attempting to repair it has complicated and frustrated improvement efforts. It is difficult to coordinate remedial action, and difficult to understand what needs to happen in order to reduce the investment in receivables.

"While 75% of CFOs make reducing days sales outstanding and improving cash flow a priority, only 25% have enough visibility into the order-to-cash process to do so", according to an AMR Research study (Hagerty, 2001). Management of the order-to-cash process as an integrated whole provides the ideal environment in which to produce the reports necessary to provide the required insight.

Gunn Partners (a leading benchmarking firm)[3] estimate that the order-to-cash process costs between 0.75 and 1% of revenue. This indicates the order of magnitude of the value-adding opportunity that is presented by the outsourcing concept.

8.4   ADDING VALUE

The order-to-cash process is the travelling companion of the cash flow cycle[4] and, as such, holds the key that can unlock precious cash resources. "Many of the policies and procedures that allow companies to extract cash from working capital are simple to understand [but]...the challenge lies in their implementation" (Payne, 2003). The act of outsourcing can break any logjam that exists in attempts to overcome a "silo mentality" that is fragmenting the order-to-cash process, inhibiting improvement.

It is possible to bring about cohesion across the whole order-to-cash process without outsourcing by, for example, introducing the "shared service centre" concept. However, the outsourcing option provides the people involved with a sense of enterprise and contribution that is difficult to match in a shared service centre.

A shared service centre is a cost centre, a burden to the enterprise, constantly harangued from all sides, required to employ minimal resources, and to tidy up transactions for all other more important "value adding" parts of the business. This is often the internal perception of a shared service centre. A perception that understandably destroys motivation and is debilitating.

On the other hand, a third-party service provider that manages the order-to-cash process as a business is considered a partner. It is expected to meet its contracted obligations and to share any cost improvements achieved. The people working for the service provider – possibly the very same people – feel empowered, motivated

---

[3] Gunn Partners – help to improve the value, relevance and effectiveness of companies' administrative functions (http://www.gunnpartners.com).
[4] The "cash flow cycle" is the time required to convert goods into cash, from the date the company pays the costs of acquisition of the goods to the date of receipt of the cash from related sales.

and valued. They are earning an income – not accumulating costs – and are able to share in the benefit from any improvements they achieve.

It is little wonder that the outsourcing of the order-to-cash process is so widely reported – through numerous case studies – to have been successful in releasing working capital from the cash flow cycle and reducing costs. Ideally any long-term strategic outsourcing of trade credit management activities should be part of an overall order-to-cash process outsourcing endeavour.

Part III
Power Blueprints – Practical Tools: The How

9

Measuring – Switch on Credit Power

9.1 THE REWARD SYSTEM IS THE LEVER

The system of rewards – explicit or implicit – that operates in an organization drives behaviour. Often though only activities and/or achievements that are measured are rewarded or punished.

The credit and receivables management activities in many firms are seen as "sales avoidance" departments, or have degenerated into mere debt collection operations, principally because their power has been shackled by an imbalance of the performance measures applied. The popular focus on the days sales outstanding (DSO), bad debts incurred, and operating costs metrics has turned many credit people away from endeavours designed to increase sales and net revenues. These three metrics alone, proclaim the message that credit should be minimized and should be reserved only for the very few obviously creditworthy customers. This is a natural reaction; avoiding granting credit reduces DSO, bad debts and costs (since less time is needed for credit analysis and collection efforts) and achieves the unspoken objectives embodied in the three metrics. However, this outcome will be out of line with overall corporate objectives. The latter are more likely to demand a balance is struck between employing the power of credit to help develop the business on the one hand, and these metrics on the other. Unless corrected, this imbalance will cause frustration within the sales team, and between the sales and credit teams.

It is clear that the power of credit can be rendered impotent by any disconnect between stated corporate objectives and the objectives communicated by the measurement and rewards system.

9.2 CONNECTING THE LEVER TO CREDIT POWER

Designing effective performance measures is a vitally important step towards achieving corporate objectives; bearing this in mind, measures must be fashioned in the context of human nature. It is essential, therefore, to institute performance measures that will motivate behaviour likely to lead to the achievement of required objectives, rather than produce unwelcome surprise results.

Credit objectives can be effectively aligned with the overall objective of maximizing total shareholder return (TSR) by introducing a balanced set of performance measures. The credit-related subset of corporate objectives includes seven specific objectives that can usefully be listed under three subsections, as follows:

- Maximizing sales or turnover (maximizing profit):
  - match the terms offered by competitors
  - provide a competitive edge
  - expand the market
- Asset management or return on capital employed (ROCE):
  - minimize the receivables balance
  - maximize cash flow received
- Controlling costs or maximizing profit:
  - minimize bad debts written off
  - minimize the cost of capital

As mentioned, most credit management performance measures address only three of these points, specifically "minimize the receivables amount", "maximize cash flow" and "minimize bad debts". The other value-adding (business development) aspects of the job require emphasis, in order to ensure they receive adequate attention.

9.2.1   Match competitors/provide competitive edge/expand the market

Performance measures in these respects should be tailored to correspond with your company's specific objectives. Some examples in relation to matching competitors, providing a competitive edge and expanding your market could be:

- Arrange "silent" payment risk cover, at a competitive cost, for sales to the state-owned buyer in Burkina Faso
- Find a bank willing to confirm LCs opened by YZ Russian Bank
- Set up an inventory financing plan to enable distributors to increase purchases by X%
- Identify three potential creditworthy customers for our product in India, before the sales team visits that country in the fourth quarter

Measuring, recognizing and rewarding this type of achievement will encourage the development of potent dynamics both within a credit team and between the credit and marketing teams. Credit employees will be encouraged to understand customer needs and market opportunities, to investigate financial markets, and to uncover appropriate financial structures and those willing to shoulder some or all of the payment risks involved. In short they will be encouraged to become outward looking, customer oriented and innovative. In this way the credit function can be transformed from a "cost centre" negative into a "contributor" positive.

9.2.2   Cost of capital

Your company's cost of capital is related to the risk perceptions of potential shareholders (stockholders) and lenders. If receivables are a significant asset, then the "risk profile" of your receivables portfolio is an important consideration. Performance measures should monitor the overall risk profile and should be targeted at maintaining a certain maximum weighted average default probability.

The cost of capital concept arises out of a study of the risk-to-reward-ratio expectations of the parties that provide business capital. Lenders (bankers) generally require an interest rate that reflects their internal assessment of the credit risk of a particular loan or financing arrangement. Bond holders and commercial paper investors usually rely on a third-party credit rating to provide a risk indication, and hence a reward (yield or interest rate) expectation. These credit risk assessments will take into account the structure of your company's balance sheet (with particular emphasis on leverage, i.e. the relative amounts of supplier credit versus interest-bearing financing versus equity), the risk inherent in the assets held (including receivables), management capabilities, business prospects and any collateral offered. Therefore – if your receivables balance is significant – the "risk profile" of your receivables portfolio will influence the cost of borrowing money to fund business operations and expansion.

Similarly, the providers of equity capital (potential stockholders or shareholders) will assess the risk that their investment may be lost, and they will demand an appropriate return. Since stockholders receive no collateral and must expect to be the last participants to be repaid – should a company fail – they will demand a higher return than "lenders". Therefore equity capital is the most expensive form of capital available.

A direct relationship between the cost of capital and the risk profile of the receivables portfolio is not widely recognized. However, this situation could change as service companies become more prominent. Service companies tend to present balance sheets evidencing relatively small amounts invested in fixed assets and relatively large receivables portfolios.

Consideration of receivable portfolio risk has also relatively recently come to prominence in the banking sector. This is due to proposals to reform the Basle Concordat and require banks to reserve capital based on the risk profile of their loan portfolios. Banks must now develop methods to evaluate the risk profile of their portfolios, in order to satisfy their respective supervisory authorities and minimize their cost of capital.

9.2.3   Receivables/cash flow/bad debts

The most prevalent credit performance measurement is "days sales outstanding" or DSO. The basic formula for calculating DSO is:

(Average Receivables) divided by (Average Sales per Day)

"Average Sales per Day" is calculated as follows:

(Annual Sales) divided by (365)

Gallinger (1995) has examined 11 different measurement techniques, including DSO, through the use of a common set of data for sales and accounts receivable. This has proved that most commonly used techniques fail to solve the "sales influence problem". The "sales influence problem" refers to the outcome that results if sales are not stable or rising from month to month. If sales drop or become erratic from month to month, or are seasonal, the resulting calculations of DSO and other popular measures are misleading and essentially useless.

It is clear that all of the traditional measurement techniques are inadequate and discredited, nevertheless credit and receivables management professionals generally maintain faith in the DSO or some derivative of this measure. There are four reasons for this:

1. Finance academics have instilled in generations of students a belief in DSO as the prime measure of effectiveness in relation to receivables, consequently this is the measure commonly required by senior executives.
2. Since some of the traditional methods work satisfactorily in times when turnover (sales) values are stable or increasing steadily month by month, they gain false credibility.
3. Computer systems have not been available to handle a better measurement system (based on individual invoices), particularly in high-volume situations.
4. If managers use a flawed system they always have a ready excuse for failing to meet their targets.

The last point is not made flippantly. Many people do not like to be measured. Hence they prefer a measurement system which can be challenged when it produces an unfavourable result. Of course DSO is seldom challenged when it produces a favourable result.

9.2.4   Sales-weighted DSO – the alternative that works

Sales-weighted DSO is calculated by relating your outstanding receivable balances directly to the sales that generated the invoices. The result of using this methodology is that a sales-weighted DSO has no "sales bias" or "sales influence problem". Therefore the result calculated for each reporting period (say monthly) can be confidently compared to all calculations for other comparable periods. A spreadsheet-based worksheet that facilitates producing a sales-weighted DSO and several other useful reports can be acquired through Dr Gallinger's website (software *Say No to DSO*; website URL: http://www.public.asu.edu/~bac524/).

10

A Practical Country Risk
Management Process

10.1 PREAMBLE

Every company that is exporting goods or services needs a systematic, cost-effective and practical internal process, designed to produce a monetary limit for its exposure to risk in each pertinent country. The process described in this chapter is the author's preferred approach. It was developed with the assistance of Y. A. Jarmain. If you decide to apply this process in practice, it should be adapted to the particular needs and circumstances of your company.

10.2 THE 11-STEP PROCESS

1. Establish the amount of your company's shareholders' own funds (equity).
2. Decide how much of your company's equity should be allocated to each category of risk from "A" (least risky) through "B", "C1", "C2", "D1", "D2" to "E" (most risky).
3. Choose a country risk rating agency from which to regularly obtain basic country risk ratings. Alternatively the ratings of several agencies could be obtained and "averaged".
4. Assign categories of risk to agency country risk ratings.
5. Decide on the list of countries important to your company's business plans, and obtain the GDP figure for each country.
6. Calculate an *initial limit* for each country, using the formula shown below.
7. Systematically consider special elements that apply to your company's industry or sector and those that apply to your company itself, in respect of each country. Assign a limit adjustment amount to each such element by applying subjective judgement.
8. Add (and/or subtract) the limit adjustment elements to (and/or from) the initial country limit, in order to establish a specific country limit appropriate for your company.
9. Consider whether the limits created in this way are sensible and practical. If necessary review and adjust some of the assumptions made or formulas applied in the model, and rework the limits.
10. Regularly gather information as to your company's risk exposure in each country

and compare this with the country limits. Take action to eliminate any exposure in excess of a particular country limit.

11. Regularly review and update country limits to take account of changes in each country's circumstances.

10.3   THE COUNTRY RISK LIMIT DECISION PROCESS EXPLAINED

10.3.1   Shareholders' equity

"Establish the amount of your company's shareholders' own funds (equity)."

The central idea behind country risk exposure management is that your company should be protected from destruction should any one country fail. A country would be said to have "failed" if your company's customers in that country were unable or unwilling to pay their debts due to the company. If a particular class of receivables were to be lost in this way, the loss would have to be covered by shareholders' equity. If your equity was insufficient, your company would face bankruptcy. Therefore the first step in deciding on country limits is to ascertain how much money is available to cover any loss; that is, to find out the amount of the shareholders' equity.

10.3.2   Risk categories and equity allocation

"Decide how much of your company's equity should be allocated to each category of risk from 'A' (least risky) through 'B', 'C1', 'C2', 'D1', 'D2' to 'E' (most risky)."

The low-risk rated countries are less likely to fail and therefore your company can afford to put at risk a large proportion of its equity, by exposure to such countries. In fact the company may be able to justify putting at risk a multiple of its capital in respect of low-risk rated countries. Conversely, your company should risk progressively smaller proportions of its equity against each successive category, as the risk of failure increases.

This may be illustrated as follows. Say a company has an equity of $100 million. Accept risk exposures as shown in Table 10.1.

Table 10.1

Risk category	Proportion (%)	Amount*
A	75	$75 million
B	50	$50 million
C1	20	$20 million
C2	10	$10 million
D1	3	$3 million
D2	1	$1 million
E	0	$0

* The total amount allocated across all risk categories will be greater than the total amount of the equity.

10.3.3   Country risk rating agency

"Choose a country risk rating agency from which to regularly obtain basic country risk ratings. Alternatively the ratings of several agencies could be obtained and 'averaged'."

There are several internationally renowned agencies that produce regular country risk analysis reports and risk ratings, for subscribers. They generally employ teams of economists and political scientists to analyse countries on the following criteria:

- Economic indicators:
  - balance of payments
  - size of external debt
  - growth in GNP
  - inflation
  - debt servicing burden
  - structure of exports
- Political factors:
  - internal stability
  - external stability
  - the analyst's "sixth-sense factor"

Each agency coalesces its analysis down to a rating for each country and each agency has its own way of expressing such ratings. Some agencies assign a score out of, say, 10, others assign a letter or series of letters or a word, for example "substandard", others assign a combination of letters and numbers.

If the various agencies' ratings were used to rank a list of countries, the ranking, would be similar for each agency, regardless of the variety of scoring methods used. This is so because all the agencies utilize similar data (data available publicly from sources such as the International Monetary Fund, World Bank and the Bank for International Settlements). Differences will arise where judgement has been applied particularly in assessing the skills of a country's officials in respect of economic management, and in assessing political factors.

It is conceivable that several ratings could be used to produce a combined or average rating for each country. However, it is unlikely that such an exercise would make sufficient difference to the overall outcome to justify the additional cost and effort involved. Hence it should be sufficient to choose any single recognized agency's risk ratings to serve as a base for your company's country risk analysis.

10.3.4   Link risk ratings with risk categories

"Assign categories of risk to agency country risk ratings."

The risk ratings of *Euromoney* have been chosen here for the purposes of illustration. *Euromoney* publishes ratings out of 100 for each country analysed. The higher the rating the lower the risk of failure and vice versa. These ratings may be translated into risk categories, for example as shown in Table 10.2.

10.3.5   Choose a list of countries

"Decide on the list of countries important to your company's business plans, and obtain the GDP figure for each country."

Table 10.2

Euromoney rating	Risk category	Proportion (%)	Amount
76–100	A	75	$75 million
60–75	B	50	$50 million
50–59	C1	20	$20 million
40–49	C2	10	$10 million
30–39	D1	3	$3 million
20–29	D2	1	$1 million
0–19	E	0	$0

This list should include all the foreign countries with which your company will transact business.

10.3.6   Calculate the initial country limit

"Calculate an *initial limit* for each country, using the formula shown below."

1. Calculate the share of equity available for each country in each risk category. This is done by dividing the equity amount allocated for "A" rated countries by the number of "A" rated countries, dividing the equity amount allocated for "B" rated countries by the number of "B" rated countries, and so on. This creates a table such as Table 10.3 which is given for illustrative purposes.
2. Decide on a "factor per risk category" to apply to each country's GDP figure, to obtain a limit indication. This could be done as shown in Table 10.4.

    GDP has been chosen here since (a) it is a figure that is generally available and comparable for all countries, and (b) it is an indication of the relative size of a country's economy. It may be argued that some other indicator should be used, such as "foreign currency reserves" for example, but this is a matter for each user of the process to decide.

    The "factor per risk category" determination method adopted here evolved from the need to reduce most countries' GDP numbers to workable figures. GDP is a superior basis for limit setting since it indicates the relative size of the economy of a country. However, GDP numbers are so large in relation to the size of "reasonable

Table 10.3

Euromoney rating	Risk category	Proportion (%)	Amount	Countries*	Equity allocation
76–100	A	75	$75 million	5	$15 million each
60–75	B	50	$50 million	10	$5 million each
50–59	C1	20	$20 million	4	$5 million each
40–49	C2	10	$10 million	2	$5 million each
30–39	D1	3	$3 million	3	$1 million each
20–29	D2	1	$1 million	4	$0.25 million each
0–19	E	0	$0	2	$0

* This is the number of countries in each risk category.

Table 10.4

Euromoney rating	Risk category	Proportion (%)	Amount	Countries	Equity allocation	Factor*
76–100	A	75%	$75 million	5	$15 million each	0.002
60–75	B	50%	$50 million	10	$5 million each	0.0018
50–59	C1	20%	$20 million	4	$5 million each	0.0015
40–49	C2	10%	$10 million	2	$5 million each	0.001
30–39	D1	3%	$3 million	3	$1 million each	0.0008
20–29	D2	1%	$1 million	4	$0.25 million each	0.0005
0–19	E	0%	$0	2	$0	0

* The "factors" utilized are decided upon by the user in an arbitrary manner. However, they should be designed to reduce the limit, resulting from their application, as the risk of failure increases in accord with the risk category scale.

country limits" that they have to be "reduced". The approach, therefore, is to reduce GDP numbers by factors that produce meaningful country limits. That is limits that are meaningful in the context of your company's circumstances.

The "factors" used here were created by proceeding on the basis of trial and error initially. A few country GDP figures were multiplied by various factors until a factor that "felt right" was determined. Unfortunately not everything can be determined on the basis of pure mathematics or statistics.

When this factor for "A" rated countries was settled, it was used as the starting point for the creation of the range (sliding scale) of factors to apply to countries with lower ratings. The objective was to reduce progressively the result of applying each successive factor, as the country rating worsened.

3. Multiply the GDP of each relevant country by the applicable factor and compare the result with the applicable per country equity allocation. The "initial country limit" is the *lesser* of these two amounts. Consider the illustrations shown in Tables 10.5(a)–(c).

10.3.7 Evaluate company-specific elements

"Systematically consider special elements which apply to your company's industry or sector and those which apply to your company itself, in respect of each country. Assign a limit adjustment amount to each such element by applying subjective judgement."

The initial country limit which is derived by using the process thus far is a generally applicable limit. Clearly it is based on information available to all parties and is not tailored specifically to the circumstances of your company. It is therefore important to consider your company's unique position vis-à-vis each country and to adjust the initial limit accordingly.

The following elements should be considered and each assigned a monetary limit value. These monetary limit values could be positive or negative, depending on whether the element assessed is thought to reduce the country risk or increase it, respectively.

Table 10.5

(a) Abu Dhabi

Euromoney rating	77.47
Risk category	A
0.002 × GDP	$69.95 million
Equity allocation	$15 million
Initial limit	*$15 million*

(b) Slovakia

Euromoney rating	57.92
Risk category	C1
0.0015 × GDP	$18 million
Equity allocation	$5 million
Initial limit	*$5 million*

(c) Estonia

Euromoney rating	49.4
Risk category	C2
0.001 × GDP	$2.5 million
Equity allocation	$5 million
Initial limit	*$2.5 million*

Elements

- *The strategic position of your goods within the country being analysed.* Are your products vital for the maintenance of good order in the country, or for the maintenance of exports? Examples of such products are pharmaceuticals, fuel, fertilizer and food. Non-essential-essentials, such as cigarettes and ingredients for beer manufacture, will be viewed similarly. Governments can be relied upon to ensure that debts due for essential and non-essential-essential goods are paid. However, non-essential goods (luxuries or goods with local substitutes) will carry a high risk of non-payment in a crisis.
- *Your company's influence with decision makers in the country.* If your company is in regular contact with decision makers in a country it will (a) have early warning of impending problems and (b) have a means to ensure that its interests, and those of other foreign creditors, are properly considered. This could reduce the country risk, which is not only in your company's best interest but also in the long-term best interests of the host country.
- *Your company's strategy in the geographic area in question.* Your business may, for example, have a branch office operating in a neighbouring country but need to increase sales, in order to cover fixed office costs. This may require an easing of credit limits to assist the building of a regional market share. Hence you may be willing to tolerate more country risk than would otherwise be indicated by your analysis.
- *The strategy of your company's competitors.* In order to compete effectively with other suppliers your company may have to increase the amount of credit made available in a particular country.

Table 10.6   Slovakia example

Euromoney rating	57.92
Risk category	C1
0.0015 × GDP	$18 million
Equity allocation	$5 million
Initial limit	*$5 million*
Adjustment	+$6 million
Country limit	*$10 million*

Note: The country limit indicated by the addition of the adjustment is $11 million ($5 million plus $6 million), but this must be restricted here to a maximum of twice the equity allocation, i.e. 2 × $5 million.

- *The availability of payment risk cover from banks and/or the credit insurance market.* If country risk cover is available it may be possible to take on "excessive" risk, while limiting exposure to a country by using various risk sharing or limiting instruments, subject to payment of the cost of such loss protection.

There must be an overall limit restriction

Note that initial limits should not be increased to amounts in excess of a certain predetermined multiple of the equity allocation for each country. That is to say that the user of this process should decide at the outset that – after an initial limit has been adjusted – it should not exceed, say, for example, twice the equity allocation for the country in question.

10.3.8   Adjust the initial limit

"Add (and/or subtract) the limit adjustment elements to (and/or from) the initial country limit, in order to establish a specific country limit appropriate for your company."

This step is illustrated by the following example. If your company is a crude oil supplier to Slovak refineries, the following adjustments may be considered to be justified:

- +$10 million, because Slovakia imports 100% of its crude requirements
- −$7 million, because your company has no contacts or influence in the country
- +$3 million, as your company has surplus production and few alternative markets

This yields a net adjustment amount of $6 million positive (see Table 10.6).

10.3.9   Overall review

"Consider whether the limits created in this way are sensible and practical. If necessary, review and adjust some of the assumptions made or formulas applied in the model, and rework the limits."

In view of the subjectivity and assumptions involved in this process it is advisable to review the list of country limits created, and to consider whether these are practical in terms of the needs of your company. The objective of the process is ultimately to protect your company from bankruptcy due to the failure of one country, and consequently the failure to collect all the receivables due by your customers in that country. Nonetheless it must be flexible enough to cope with changed circumstances, and it must not hamper the conduct of good-quality business. Hence the need for an overall review of the results of the process from time to time.

All country limits recommended as a result of this process should be confirmed by a senior company executive authorized by the Board of Directors.

10.3.10   Monitor and manage exposure

"Regularly gather information as to your company's risk exposure in each country and compare this with the country limits. Take action to eliminate any exposure in excess of a particular country limit."

This is the most important part of this process since it is through this step that your company's country exposures are actively managed. Your company's accounting system must be designed to produce a regular report (perhaps weekly) which shows an analysis of receivables outstanding by country. If a particular receivable is secured by a party resident in another country (a bank or parent company), the country designation of that receivable should be changed to that of the guarantor. Other company exposures within the listed countries could be added to such a report. Consignment inventory (stock) in a foreign country is an example of the type of exposure that could be added.

Comparing such a report to the country limits will highlight excess exposures so that action can be taken to transfer risks to other countries (by obtaining credit insurance or bank guarantees) or to limit (redirect) business activities.

10.3.11   Review and update limits

"Regularly review and update country limits to take account of changes in each country's circumstances."

The situation in each country is dynamic and subject to rapid change. In addition countries are interdependent so a change which affects one will affect many, often in different ways. Nevertheless changes are often subtle so it is necessary to be constantly alert. Positive changes are as important to note as negative changes. Positive changes bring with them opportunities to do more business and to outclass the competition.

Individual country limits should be reviewed formally at least twice every year and on an impromptu basis if important developments occur. It is therefore imperative that a person or persons within your company must be given the responsibility to undertake regular reviews, and to monitor developments in all relevant countries on a daily basis. The latter task should be accomplished through giving attention to the news media, through conversations with agents, banks and colleagues and through personal visits.

11

Two Practical Bank
Risk Management Processes

11.1 PREAMBLE

Every bank that provides your company with payment security (a guarantee or LC) or confirms an LC must be assessed as to its ability to meet its commitment. This is also true of any bank that is entrusted with company money or marketable securities, as investments or as collateral or for safekeeping.

The two methods described in this chapter ultimately reference the analysed bank's capital when formulating a recommended exposure limit. However, there is a body of opinion that argues persuasively against the use of a bank's capital as a yardstick in deriving an exposure limit. Supporters of this contrary view rightly point to the fact that the main reasons for bank failures are (a) poor management strategy or (b) poor management control, both of which bear no relation to capital. Consequently it is suggested that "profitability" is the preferred reference point, since it is a better indicator of a bank's performance over the whole range of its business activities. Yet there are recent examples of poor management strategies and/or lack of controls having led to spectacular profits being reported, in the short term, when market conditions happened to be favourable. Of course when market conditions turned against such strategies, those same practices led the banks into an abyss.

Think for a moment about the spectacular profits being reported by some Russian banks before they imploded during the August 1998 crises. Another pertinent example is the case involving Allied Irish Bank (AIB) and the losses it suffered as a result of poor controls. It is legitimate to consider using profits as a starting point for the calculation of a limit, but profits are too easy to manipulate in the short term and too volatile to provide a reliable foundation. Anyway, profits do feed through to capital as they are added to reserves (net of dividends) year after year.

Capital is a preferred reference point for determination of the quantum of a bank limit for the following reasons:

- Capital is a fair indicator of the relative size of a bank, in relation to its peers.
- Capital is used as the yardstick against which the Basel Committee of Bank Supervisors (followed by supervisors in over 100 countries) measure a bank's capacity to deal with the risks that it faces in the course of its day-to-day business. Hence the structure of the 1988 Capital Accord and the proposed

structure of the New Capital Accord, the so-called Basel II, that is under discussion.

• Capital is more difficult to manipulate than profit.

However, it is difficult to support the simplistic limit model provided in the five-step process presented in this chapter. A sliding scale of just 10%, then 9%, then 8% of capital is not adequate to meet the needs of many companies.

On the other hand, it is easy to defend a limit model that provides for exposures based on multiples of capital – for highly rated banks – with a sliding scale down to diminishing proportions of capital – for lesser rated banks. The second process presented includes a rating scale as part of the Bank Credit ScoreCard. The bank being rated using this alternative method is recommended a limit based on its capital divided by its risk rating. Hence an AAA bank, one that achieves a rating of between 0.5 and 0.74, is recommended a limit of between twice its capital and 1.35 times its capital. While a BB rated bank, one that achieves a rating of between 3.5 and 3.74, is recommended a limit of between 28.5 and 26.7% of its capital.

Since banks are "allowed" to take on risk-adjusted liabilities up to a multiple of their capital (12.5 times their capital in terms of the 8% rule) it must be acceptable to set limits as a multiple of capital, after adjusting to allow for the degree of perceived risk.

11.2   THE FIVE-STEP PROCESS

1. Determine whether the bank is acceptable as a payment security provider.
   1.1 This should be achieved by reference to the "rating" given to the bank by one of the recognized international bank rating agencies.
   1.2 Alternatively your company should obtain a satisfactory "credit reference" from a known and trusted second bank, generally called a "correspondent bank".
2. Establish the amount of the capital of the bank, that is, the amount of the equity plus reserves.
3. Decide a factor to apply to the amount of the bank's capital, in order to determine the "risk limit".
4. Regularly gather information as to your company's risk exposure in respect of each bank and compare this with the approved bank limits. Take action to eliminate any exposure excesses.
5. Regularly review and update bank limits to take account of changed circumstances.

11.3   THE FIVE-STEP BANK LIMIT DECISION PROCESS EXPLAINED

11.3.1   Determine the acceptability of the bank

"Determine whether a bank is acceptable as a payment security provider."

This should be achieved by reference to the "rating" given to the bank by one of the recognized international bank rating agencies. A publication called *The Bankers'*

Almanac (published by Reed Business Information Limited, http://www.reedinfo.co.uk) is one of several that provide a bank analyst with basic information about most international banks, including their credit ratings where these exist. Bank ratings can also be obtained from rating agency internet websites: FitchRatings (http://www.fitchibca.com), Moody's Investors Service (http://www.moodys.com/), and Standard and Poor's (http://www.sandp.com). In early 2003, for example, Société Générale (France) had the following credit ratings:

FitchRatings: F1+

Moody's: P-1

Standard & Poor's: AA/A-1+

Where two ratings are shown (for example AA/A-1+), the first rating (AA in this case) is the "long-term rating" which indicates the rating agency's assessment of the bank's ability to repay debt obligations with an original maturity of more than one year. The second rating (A-1+ in this case) is the "short-term rating" which indicates the rating agency's assessment of the bank's ability to repay punctually senior debt obligations with an original maturity of one year or less. It is the *short-term ratings* that are of interest in terms of this process.

Unfortunately each rating agency has its own way of describing its ratings. It is important for you to decide which rating is the lowest acceptable rating in the case of each rating agency. The following lists illustrate this point.

FitchRatings: international short-term ratings

> F1 = "Highest credit quality..." (the best available)
>
> F2
>
> F3 = "Fair credit quality...
>
>> adequate capacity for timely payment of commitments"
>
> B
>
> C = "High default risk..."
>
> D = (the worst rating in this category)

(It is submitted that banks rated F3 or better by FitchRatings are acceptable.)

Moody's Investors Service: short-term bank deposit ratings

P-1 (Prime-1) = "Superior credit quality..." (the best)

P-2

P-3 = "An acceptable credit quality and adequate capacity for timely payment..."

NP (Not Prime) = (the worst rating in this category)

(It is submitted that banks rated P-3 or better by Moody's are acceptable.)

Standard & Poor's (S&P): issuer credit rating (short-term)

A-1 = "Strong capacity to meet its financial commitments..." (the best)

A-2

A-3 = "Adequate capacity to meet its financial commitments..."

B

C

R

SD

D = (the worst rating in this category)

(It is submitted that banks rated A-3 or better by Standard & Poor's are acceptable.)

It should be noted that rating agencies may change their ratings whenever new information is received. Therefore it is prudent to obtain up-to-date information by contacting a rating agency direct, or through viewing its website.

Alternatively your company should obtain a satisfactory "credit reference" from a known and trusted second bank, generally called a "correspondent bank". All banks that operate internationally do so through the use of a network of correspondent banks. "Correspondent banks" are foreign banks with which a bank formally corresponds either by operating clearing and other accounts, or simply by exchanging signature lists and "test key" arrangements (telex or SWIFT[1] message authentication arrangements).

In cases where a local correspondent bank of good standing holds the account of another bank, it will have undertaken a due diligence check on the other bank, to ensure that it is properly constituted and supervised. In addition, in cases where it incurs any credit exposure, the correspondent bank will have assessed the ability and ethics of the other bank's management and shareholders as well as its financial condition. Local correspondent banks are therefore a useful source of information upon which your company can base a decision as to whether to accept a non-credit-rated bank as a payment security provider.

The *Bankers' Almanac* usually lists the main correspondent banks of each bank included in its main directory. Alternatively most banks will supply a list of correspondent banks to your company upon receipt of a request, or will list correspondent banks on their website.

It is advisable to approach a trusted correspondent bank with which your company has a relationship of some kind and establish whether it:

● Knows the bank in question to be properly constituted, professionally managed and well respected

---

[1] SWIFT is the Society for Worldwide Interbank Financial Telecommunication. It manages a closed private network for secure electronic communications between over 7000 financial institutions, operating in 198 countries. It is owned by the user institutions (http://www.swift.com).

- Is prepared to grant that bank unsecured (non-collateralized) credit facilities either by way of LC confirmations or otherwise

It is submitted that *if both of these questions are answered positively*, the bank in question may be accepted as a payment security provider.

11.3.2   Bank's own funds

"Establish the amount of the capital of the bank; that is, the amount of the equity plus reserves."

The *Bankers' Almanac* reports a summary of the latest financial information available from the banks included in its directory. If such information is not available from this source or the website of the bank in question, the bank should be requested to supply a copy of its latest audited annual report and accounts. Alternatively a correspondent bank may be willing to supply you with a copy of the report and accounts.

It was reported in January 1996 that the following figures appeared on the Consolidated Balance Sheet of Société Générale (France) as at 31 December 1994:

> Capital FFr (French francs) 15 103 million plus
>
> Subordinated loans FFr 29 919 million plus
>
> (note that "subordinated loans" may be considered part of "own funds")
>
> Reserves FFr 36 253 million
>
> Equals total own funds of FFr 81 275 million

This is equivalent to *total own funds of about US$15.23 billion* when translated at a rate of FFr 5.3367 equals US$1.

It was also reported that the following figures appeared on the balance sheet of United Overseas Bank SA (Geneva)[2] as at 31 December 1994:

> Capital SwFr (Swiss francs) 105 million plus
>
> Reserves SwFr 254 million plus
>
> Profit balance SwFr 25 million
>
> Equals total own funds of SwFr 384 million

This is equivalent to *total own funds of about US$293 million* when translated at a rate of SwFr 1.3086 equals US$1.

11.3.3   Decide a factor

"Decide a factor to apply to the amount of the bank's capital, in order to determine the 'risk limit'."

The factor to be applied is a matter of judgement and should be reviewed from time to time in light of your company's experience. It may also have to be applied flexibly on a case-by-case basis, taking into account specific circumstances applicable.

---

[2] United Overseas Bank SA (Geneva) later changed its name to United European Bank SA and was subsequently merged with BNP Paribas (Suisse) SA.

Nevertheless a standard factor which will accommodate most circumstances is a useful tool; for example, it may be decided to utilize a factor of 10%. This could be refined by adopting a sliding scale of, say, 10% for A-1 rated banks, 9% for A-2 banks, and 8% for A-3 banks or non-rated but acceptable banks (using the S&P rating scale as an example).

Application of the appropriate factors to the "own funds" totals shown above yields the following bank risk limits:

Société Générale (France):

> US$1523 million (being US$15.23 billion multiplied by 10%)

United Overseas Bank SA (Geneva):

> US$23.44 million (being US$293 million multiplied by 8%)

In the case of United Overseas Bank SA (Geneva), which was not rated, it may have been decided that a larger factor could safely be applied because this bank was ultimately owned by two large and powerful banks, namely Banque Nationale de Paris and Dresdner Bank AG.

11.3.4   Monitor and manage exposure

"Regularly gather information as to your company's risk exposure in respect of each bank and compare this with the bank limits. Take action to eliminate any exposure excesses."

This is the most important part of the process since it is through this step that your company's bank exposures are actively managed. Your company's accounting system must be designed to produce a regular report (perhaps weekly) that shows an analysis of payment risk security held, per bank. Other company exposures to the listed banks, such as money market deposits, derivative transactions and/or forward foreign exchange contracts, could be added to such a report.

Comparing this report with the approved bank limits will highlight excess exposures. Subsequently action should be taken to transfer excess risks to other banks (by obtaining a second bank confirmation or counter-guarantee) or to limit business activities where necessary.

11.3.5   Review and update limits

"Regularly review and update bank limits to take account of changed circumstances."

The financial and management strength of each bank is dynamic and subject to rapid change. In addition banks are interdependent so that a change that affects one will affect many, often in different ways. Nevertheless changes are often subtle so it is necessary to be constantly alert.

Positive changes are as important to note as negative changes. Positive changes bring with them opportunities to do more business and to overcome the competition. This may, for example, take the form of reducing the costs related to a series of transactions by eliminating the need to pay a second bank for LC confirmations.

Individual bank limits should be reviewed formally at least twice every year and on an unplanned basis if important developments come to the notice of your company. It is therefore imperative that a person or persons within your company must be given the responsibility to undertake regular reviews, and to monitor developments in respect of all relevant banks, on a daily basis. The latter task should be accomplished through giving attention to the news media, conversations with other banks and colleagues, and through personal visits to major banking centres.

11.4   A BANK CREDIT SCORECARD – BALANCED ANALYSIS

A Bank Credit ScoreCard is offered here as an alternative to the five-step process. It consists of a series of questions under four subheadings, namely "bank rating and financial information", "management ability and integrity", "relationship with your company", and "country risk". Certain alternative answers are possible for each question. Each answer has a score associated. These raw scores are weighted and adjusted using simple formulas to produce a bank risk score that feeds into a bank exposure limit model.

The ScoreCard can be set up on a spreadsheet without the need to use any complex programming skills. However, in order for an analyst to complete the ScoreCard competently it will be necessary to research the bank being analysed and to obtain certain basic facts. This will become clear as the questions are reviewed.

The particular questions used in this exercise were chosen using the following criteria:

- A question must (as far as possible) be capable of being answered by reference to objective information. In other words everyone in possession of the relevant facts should choose the same answer to the question.
- Only the most significant questions should be utilized. The list should be strictly limited in order to ensure that each answer, one way or the other, actually influences the overall score. If too many questions are included in a ScoreCard, each question has very little impact on the final outcome. In fact many answers cancel each other out, leading to production of a mediocre score that is essentially useless for the purpose. The purpose is to provide a clear and understandable basis on which to make a decision.
- The questions should adequately represent all aspects considered important in making a decision. They should provide the necessary balance to ensure that consideration of financial information reporting past performance does not smother consideration of non-numeric factors. The latter have been proved time and again to be the more likely cause of difficulties, poor management being the most obvious peril not apparent from a usual financial analysis.
- Questions should attempt to replicate the thought processes of highly experienced analysts, in order to produce standardized results of premium quality.

Section One: Bank rating and financial information

Q1:	What is the bank rating agency score?	200
	Enter the score related to the bank's rating according to the analysis shown in Table 11.1. Example: A-1 rating equals score of 200.	
Q2:	How recent is the financial information? <6 months old = 20; <1 year old = 10; <18 months old = 5; older = 0	20
	The older the available annual report, the lower the score. Example: financial information less than 6 months old equals score of 20.	
Q3:	What is the bank's equity? >10% of the proposed limit = 80; >8% = 60; >6% = 40; less = 0	80
	The benchmark set by the Basel Capital Accord requires banks to have capital equivalent to at least 8% of their weighted liabilities. This question scores the bank according to the relationship between the bank's capital and the limit that your company proposes or needs to record for this bank. In this example, say, the bank's capital exceeds 10% of the proposed limit, that means a score of 80 is awarded.	

Subsection score (actual/converted)	300	1.00

The actual subsection score – called X in the formula – is converted as follows:

$$Xc = 20/(X/15)$$

Ultimately this ScoreCard will produce a bank score ranging from 0.50 (lowest risk of default) upward, with a score of more than 5 indicating an unacceptably high risk of default.

Table 11.1   Score per bank rating

Standard & Poor's	Moody's	Fitch	Score
A-1	Prime-1	F1	200
A-2	Prime-2	F2	160
A-3	Prime-3	F3	120
B	—	B	60
C and worse	Not prime	C and worse	0

Section Two: Management ability and integrity

Q4:   How many years has bank been in business? >15 years = 20; >7   20
years = 10; less = 0

If it is accepted that economic cycles repeat every seven years, a bank
that has survived in business through at least two cycles has proved the
necessary organizational resilience. Example: bank in business for more
than 15 years equals a score of 20.

Q5:   Is the bank managed by officers of a significant transnational financial   20
services group, under management contract? Yes = 20; No = 0

Often subsidiaries in emerging markets are "localized" (sold to
local investors) but continue to be managed by seconded employees
from their original owner. The skill and support available to management has an important influence on the inherent risk. Example answer is
"yes" equals score of 20.

Q6:   Has there been any scandal in the past two years? No = 20; Yes = 0   40
Has there been any "dispute" with the authorities in the last two years?
No = 20; Yes = 0

This is an attempt to factor management integrity into the score. The
argument is that if management lack integrity this will be signalled by
the occurrence of disputes (e.g. alleged failure to remit duties collected)
or scandals (e.g. employees injured due to unsafe conditions). The
question requires a no or yes answer to each question. No = 20 but
Yes = 0. There is no provision for a bank with just a little scandal to
earn some points, any scandal equals zero points. The objective is to
elicit an answer that makes a difference to the overall result, even after it
is mingled with the other answers. In this example accept there was no
scandal and no dispute, hence a score of 20 + 20.

Q7:   Is the bank a member of a significant transnational financial services   80
group (meaning >50% owned)? Yes = 80; No = 0

The expectation is that the owner will exercise management controls,
including internal audits and the imposition of tried and tested
procedures. This will considerably reduce risks related to poor
management and poor controls. Example: score 80.

Q8:   Does the bank carry the name of a significant transnational financial   40
services group? Yes = 40; No = 0

Again the expectation is that the transnational bank will exercise even
more close control over its local operation if its brand reputation is at
risk. Example: score 40.

Subsection score (actual/converted)   200   1.00

The actual subsection score – called Y in the formula – is converted as follows:

$$Yc = 40/(Y/5)$$

Section Three: Relationship with your company

Q9: Does your company have an active relationship with this bank or the related bank group? Yes = 50; No = 0	50

The rationale for including this question (an easy one to answer) is that if problems arise your company should have a better ability to secure a solution if a relationship exists beyond the transaction at issue. Again this question calls for a simple yes or no, there is no provision allowed for a partial score to be awarded. The result must be 50 points or zero. In this example score 50.

Subsection score (actual/converted)   50   1.00

The actual subsection score – called Z in the formula – is converted as follows:

$$Zc = 20/(Z/2.5)$$

Section Four: Country risk

Q10: Is the bank based in an OECD member country? Yes = 100 (and other questions in this section = 0); No = 0   100

If the bank is based in an OECD[3] member country, enter a score of 100 and this section will be complete. However, if it is not, enter zero and answer the next two questions, i.e. Q11 and Q12. *If the bank is based in your country* answer "yes" to this question even if your country is not a member of the OECD. For this example answer "yes" equals a score of 100.

Q11: What is the FitchRatings' long-term foreign currency sovereign rating? AAA/AA = 60; A/BBB = 50; BB = 40; B = 30; CCC = 20; CC = 10; C/D = 0   0

These ratings were chosen because they are available on the FitchRatings website (http://www.fitchibca.com).

Q12: What is the host country production of the product you are exporting as a percentage of host country consumption? <25% = 40; <50% = 30; <75% = 20; more = 0   0

It is suggested that "country risk" is reduced to the extent that the product that you are exporting cannot be substituted by local production, in the host country. Relevant statistics are usually available from the websites of international non-government agencies such as the International Monetary Fund or the World Bank.

Subsection score (actual/converted)   100   1.00

The actual subsection score – called R in the formula – is converted as follows:

$$R_c = 20/(R/5)$$

[3] OECD – the Organization for Economic Cooperation and Development (http://www.oecd.org) had 30 member countries as of the first quarter of 2003, as follows: Australia, Austria, Belgium, Canada, Czech Republic, Denmark, Finland, France, Germany, Greece, Hungary, Iceland, Ireland, Italy, Japan, Korea, Luxembourg, Mexico, the Netherlands, New Zealand, Norway, Poland, Portugal, Slovak Republic, Spain, Sweden, Switzerland, Turkey, United Kingdom, United States.

Section Five: Selected score exaggerator

Add together the scores from Q1, Q3, Q6, Q7 and the Section Four total then enter the sum here	500

> In this example, add Q1 = 200 plus Q3 = 80 plus Q6 = 40 plus Q7 = 80 plus Section Four = 100, making a sum total of 500.
> The original ScoreCard failed to sufficiently discriminate between low-risk, medium-risk and high-risk banks. This section was added in order to correct that flaw. The five items selected here are considered to be those that would each be a potential "roadblock", in the minds of experienced credit analysts. Therefore each such factor carries more weight if it is negative than it does if it is positive.

Subsection score (actual/converted)	500	5.00

The actual subsection score – called E in the formula – is converted as follows:

$$Ec = (500/E)^*(5^*((500/E)^2))$$

The effect of this formula is to increase the subsection converted score exponentially, if the actual score (the sum of the five chosen individual scores) decreases. This effectively increases the overall score – indicating higher risk of default – thus discriminating between good, indifferent and bad banks.

Overall bank risk score	0.50

The overall bank risk score is calculated by adding together the five converted scores and dividing that total by 18. The formula is $= (Xc + Yc + Zc + Rc + Ec)/18$.

The denominator was arrived at simply as the number required to produce the target minimum possible score of 0.5.

11.5   A BANK EXPOSURE LIMIT MODEL AND INTERNAL RATING SCHEME

This bank exposure limit model complements the Bank Credit ScoreCard described in the previous section. The overall bank risk score produced by the ScoreCard is used to calculate one element of the model, and can be used to produce an internal credit rating. The latter will be useful in terms of portfolio analysis and portfolio risk management, in relation to bank exposure.

11.5.1   Rules of the bank limit model

The model consists of three restrictive parameters:

1. The limit must not exceed a certain prescribed proportion of your company's equity – say 20% – in order to regulate concentration risk.
2. The limit must not exceed the amount required to accommodate normal business requirements. This amount can be forecast in consultation with marketing and treasury colleagues, based on planned activity.
3. The limit must not exceed the amount calculated according to the formula: *(Bank's Equity) divided by (Overall Bank Risk Score)*. This formula effectively scales down the potential limit as the score indicates increasing risk of default. It also ensures

that any limit will be suitably adjusted automatically, whenever the ScoreCard is updated with fresh information.

11.5.2   Internal bank credit rating conversion chart

Suggested credit rating equivalents in relation to various overall bank risk scores produced by the ScoreCard are shown in Table 11.2:

Table 11.2

Score	Rating
0.50–0.74	AAA
0.75–0.99	AA+
1.00–1.24	AA
1.25–1.49	AA−
1.50–1.74	A+
1.75–1.99	A
2.00–2.24	A−
2.25–2.49	BBB+
2.50–2.74	BBB
2.75–2.99	BBB−
3.00–3.24	BB+
3.25–3.49	BB
3.50–3.74	BB−
3.75–3.99	B+
4.00–4.24	B
4.25–4.49	B−
4.50–4.74	CCC+
4.75–4.99	CCC
5.00–5.25	CCC−
Higher	D

12
Promissory Notes and Demand Guarantees

12.1 INTRODUCTION

Documentary credits or letters of credit (LCs) issued under International Chamber of Commerce (ICC) Uniform Customs and Practice for Documentary Credits publication number 500 (UCP 500) rules are a useful way to provide some payment security, while also affording the buyer an element of protection. Nevertheless they have some drawbacks that make it worthwhile to consider alternatives. These drawbacks include:

(a) They are relatively costly.
(b) They are inflexible.
(c) They require the participation of a bank in the processing of the transaction.

The "step by step" customer relationship management approach to payment security – which means moving from a position of full security, for customer and country risk, to a desired position of a mixture of open account and payment security – makes it necessary to find more flexible arrangements. The alternatives considered here are based on the use of a combination of promissory notes (PNs) and demand guarantees (DGs), or demand guarantees alone.

12.2 PROMISSORY NOTES (PNs)

In this context PNs are made subject to English law and jurisdiction – that is to say, subject to the Bills of Exchange Act 1882 which defines a PN as:

> An unconditional promise in writing, made by one person to another, signed by the maker, engaging to pay, on demand, or at a fixed or determinable future time, a sum certain in money, to, or to the order of, a specified person, or to bearer. (See Appendix 12.1)

12.3 DEMAND GUARANTEES (DGs)

DGs are usually made subject to the Uniform Rules for Demand Guarantees (URDG) of the ICC (publication number 458). A DG can either be issued by a bank in conjunction with a PN (see Appendix 12.2) or without the use of a PN (see Appendix 12.3).

12.4   ALTERNATIVE ONE

Where payment risk cover is only provided for 30 days between the delivery date and the due date, the procedure is as follows:

- Contract of sale/purchase is agreed. Contract includes agreement that:
  - seller will immediately provide a proforma invoice based on 110% of the contract quantity at the current mean reference price plus or minus the agreed premium or discount. This proforma invoice will show a mutually agreed "estimated due date" – usually the last day of the expected delivery date range plus 30 days.
  - buyer will create a PN for the amount of the proforma invoice, payable on the fifth day after the "estimated due date", and place it in the custody of a bank, as instructed by the seller.
  - in all other respects "open account" arrangements will apply and the PN will become null and void if the invoice is paid on due date.
- Proforma invoice is issued.
- PN is created and handed to the designated local bank.
- Delivery of the commodity is authorized by the seller.
- Actual quantities and the price calculation are agreed between buyer and seller.
- Final invoice is issued.
- Discussion between buyer and seller takes place to agree whether or not it is necessary to exchange the existing PN for a new PN, which shows the true amount due and a due date five days after the actual due date.
- If a new PN is issued, it is exchanged for the original PN.
- On due date the invoice amount is paid by the buyer or the buyer's designated bank, direct to the seller. Then the PN becomes null and void.
- If the invoice is not paid, the PN is presented on its due date, that is, about five days after the invoice due date.

This arrangement enables the seller to decide how much buyer risk and/or country risk to share with a bank. If the seller wishes to limit its payment risk, a bank can be asked to cover up to 100% of the amount of the PN, for a fee. The seller can choose a foreign bank or a local bank, thereby choosing whether to cover the country risk or not, respectively. The selected bank would issue a DG in favour of the seller (see Appendix 12.2). The seller would expect to pay a guarantee fee relating to the:

(a) Risks that are covered.
(b) Extent of cover (80 or 90 or 100%, for example).
(c) Number of days the guarantee will be outstanding.

The buyer would not pay any fee.

   The buyer's line of credit with the bank which issues a DG will be reduced by the amount of the DG for as long as it is outstanding. A DG would be written to expire five days after the due date of the related PN.

12.5   ALTERNATIVE TWO

This covers the scenario where a bank provides payment risk cover for the first 30 days after delivery *and* then goes on to provide the buyer with finance for 90 or 120 days thereafter. That is to say, where a bank pays the seller after 30 days but the buyer only pays the bank 120 or 150 days after delivery.

- In this case the transaction is initially processed and secured as described in Section 12.4 Alternative One above, except:
  - the PN is made payable to the financing bank (this must be a mutually acceptable bank).
  - necessary approvals for foreign borrowing must be obtained from the Central Bank and/or Ministry of Finance, if applicable.
  - the purchase/sale contract must be assigned to the bank by the buyer – with the seller's consent.
- On or before the 30th day after the delivery date the estimated PN will be replaced by a PN which incorporates the actual amount due, an appropriate interest clause and a due date being 120 or 150 days after the delivery date, as applicable.
- On the 30th day after the delivery date the bank pays the seller in full.
- On the 120th or 150th day after the delivery date the buyer pays the bank an amount equal to the cost of the commodity plus interest, at the agreed rate, for the period of finance.

This scenario potentially carries the same advantages as Alternative One but with the following additional considerations:

1. An underlying loan agreement between the buyer and the bank is required. This provides the bank with security in the transaction itself and thereby yields the potential to minimize the cost of borrowing.
2. A wider foreign bank credit base can be accessed because the prime bank can syndicate the funding of such a loan. Thus the buyer can become favourably known to a wider community of banks.
3. This scenario prepares the buyer for a direct commercial paper and/or capital market issue programme at some later date.

12.6   RISK CONSIDERATIONS

There is an additional risk to consider when choosing to use promissory notes and/or demand guarantees instead of documentary credits.

12.6.1   Buyer's point of view

If a buyer accepts the arrangements outlined in Alternatives One or Two above, an additional risk becomes apparent and must be considered. This risk is the "risk of unjustified presentation or calling". In other words, with the PN or DG in place before delivery, it is possible for a dishonest seller to fail to deliver but still claim payment, and be paid. It is up to the buyer to judge whether this is a significant risk, by taking account of the reliability and integrity of the seller.

Insurance may be available to protect the buyer from the risk that the seller may present the PN for payment, or call for payment under the DG, even though the seller has not delivered the products.

APPENDIX 12.1

PROMISSORY NOTE FORMAT

____ (place of issue) ____ the ____ (date) ____ for ____ (amount in figures) ____

On the ____ (due date) ____ I/we promise to pay, against this Promissory Note, to the order of ____ (seller or designated bank) ____ the amount of ____ (amount in words) ____.

Payment due under contract number ____ (contract number) ____ dated ____ (date) ____.

This Promissory Note is subject to English law and jurisdiction.
Payable without any deduction for and free of any tax, impost, levy or duty of any nature, present or future.

Payable at:
(name and address of Paying Bank)

(name of Buyer)

Authorized Signature(s)

COMPLETED EXAMPLE PROMISSORY NOTE:

London the First day of April 2004 for Euro 25 000 000

On the First day of May 2004 we promise to pay, against this Promissory Note, to the order of ABC Sugar Exporters SA the amount of Twenty Five Million Euro.

Payment due under contract number 123678 dated 17 March 2004.

This Promissory Note is subject to English law and jurisdiction.
Payable without any deduction for and free of any tax, impost, levy or duty of any nature, present or future.

Payable at:
XYZ Bank Plc
London

Sugar Importers Limited

Harry Jones

Authorized Signature(s)

APPENDIX 12.2

DEMAND GUARANTEE FORMAT

Date

Supplier name and address

OUR REFERENCE:_____

With reference to your contract number __ (number) __ dated __ (date) __ with __ (Buyer) __ their reference __ (number) __ for sale of __ (product) __ we __ (Bank) __ irrevocably commit to honour a promissory note payable at the counters of __ (Bank) __ in the amount of USD __ (amount) __ (United States Dollars __ (words) __) issued by __ (Buyer) __ under the said contract and duly endorsed (without recourse) by you in our favour and maturing no later than __ (date) __ , provided the said promissory note is accompanied by the following documents:

A)   Your signed written statement that the amount of the accompanying promissory note represents the net amount due by the Buyer in respect of the referenced contract between the Buyer and you and that the invoice, mentioned in 'B' below, having been duly presented for payment, remains unpaid five (5) calendar days after due date.

B)   Copy of the invoice for the amount claimed in 'A' above (telex copy acceptable).

Should the value of the promissory note under the above contract, be paid to you prior to the maturity of the promissory note, then the promissory note shall automatically become null and void, and our commitment to honour such promissory note will also be automatically extinguished.

This commitment expires at the counters of __ (Bank) __ on __ (date) __ and any claims under this commitment must be presented before expiry.

This commitment is subject to the Uniform Rules for Demand Guarantees of the International Chamber of Commerce (publication number 458).

Signed __(name) ___

....

Authorized Signature

APPENDIX 12.3

DEMAND GUARANTEE FORMAT
(NO PROMISSORY NOTE)

Date

Supplier name and address

OUR REFERENCE:_____

With reference to your contract number __ (number) __ dated __ (date) __ with __ (Buyer) __ their reference __ (number) __ for sale of __ (product) __ we __ (Bank) __ irrevocably commit to pay you the amount due under the said contract subject to a maximum of USD __ (amount) __ (United States Dollars __ (words) __) on presentation of your simple demand accompanied by the following documents:

A)   Your signed written statement that the amount of the accompanying simple demand represents the net amount due by the Buyer in respect of the referenced contract between the Buyer and you and that the invoice, mentioned in 'B' below, having been duly presented for payment, remains unpaid five (5) calendar days after due date.

B)   Copy of the invoice for the amount claimed in 'A' above (telex copy acceptable).

This commitment expires at the counters of __ (Bank) __ on __ (date) __ and any claims under this commitment must be presented before expiry.

This commitment is subject to the Uniform Rules for Demand Guarantees of the International Chamber of Commerce (publication number 458).

Signed __(name) __

....

Authorized Signature

13

Payment Undertakings and
Risk Sharing in Practice

13.1 INTRODUCTION

The payment undertaking based arrangement described in this chapter offers a viable and flexible alternative to payment security based on either:

- Documentary credits (including standby LCs), or
- Buyer's bank guarantees, or
- Promissory notes

Payment undertakings are also sometimes called purchase confirmations. They ask no more of the buyer than a simple but separate confirmation that the buyer will fulfil the terms of the contract with the seller. A payment undertaking does not impose any additional burden over and above that already agreed in the purchase/sale contract. It is, however, a separate formal irrevocable document, usually addressed directly to a bank designated by the seller.

In preparation for this type of arrangement the relevant purchase/sale contract must contain the following two clauses:

> Credit: At least five days prior to delivery Buyer will send to Seller's bank, with a copy to Seller's financial contact, a payment undertaking in a format acceptable to Seller (bank details and payment undertaking text will be provided).

and

> Assignment: This agreement will not be assignable by either party without the written consent of the other, which shall not be unreasonably withheld. However, in the event payment is not made by the buyer on due date, seller has the right to assign the financial rights under this agreement to a bank without the prior consent of the buyer.

13.2 HISTORICAL DEVELOPMENT OF PAYMENT UNDERTAKINGS

Businesses that specialize in oil trading (traders) usually have a limited financial asset or capital base since their main assets are the skills and contacts of their executives. They therefore had difficulty establishing significant documentary credit facilities with international banks.

When a trader participated in "back-to-back" deals (see box) in terms of which, for instance, it bought a cargo of crude oil from an oil producer that required it to provide documentary credit (LC) payment security, a mechanism was needed to enable an international bank to open the LC for the trader. Normally the trader would immediately sell the same cargo to a highly creditworthy oil company (oil major), but since the oil major (ultimate buyer) would not normally provide an LC in favour of the trader, a bank could not operate a traditional "back-to-back" LC arrangement. Hence an alternative mechanism was needed to enable a bank to open the necessary LC for the trader.

> A *"back-to-back" LC arrangement* is one in terms of which a bank opens an LC that emulates the terms and conditions of an LC received by its customer. The terms and conditions of each must be sufficiently similar to enable the bank to reimburse itself, when it has paid out under its own LC, by presenting documents and collecting payment under the received LC. The bank handles all the documents related to both transactions and thereby secures its position, provided no mistakes are made in the text of its own LC and/or in handling the related documents. In this way the bank incurs "documentary risk" rather than "customer payment risk" and is therefore able to open LCs for financially weak customers that act as intermediaries.

Some international banks found a way to do this using payment undertakings and consequently assisted in the expansion of international trade, and in the safe expansion of their own business activity. This is achieved by asking an oil major (ultimate buyer) to issue a payment undertaking direct to the trader's bank, irrevocably undertaking (a) to pay for the cargo, if it is delivered as agreed in the purchase/sale contract, and (b) to route the payment directly to the account of the trader at that specific bank, provided the trader's invoice contains details of that specific bank.

This simple device enables the LC issuing bank to control the receipt of the funds from the oil major and the payment to the seller (producer) under the LC, utilizing those same funds less the trader's gross margin. This permits such banks to open LCs that they could not otherwise open.

The use of the payment undertaking methodology has since been expanded to provide an alternative method of covering general payment risk where no intermediary parties (traders) are involved. It has, for example, proved popular in relation to buyers situated in the Czech Republic, Hungary, Poland, Nigeria and Angola, as an alternative which is more flexible and cost effective than the use of either documentary credits or bank guarantees.

Using the payment undertaking method banks now cover (underwrite) direct corporate payment risk through agreements with sellers. Such agreements are generally not disclosed to the buyers, but the buyers are required to provide payment undertakings. In some cases the seller formally assigns the proceeds of the sale to the bank before delivery of the contracted goods or services. In these cases the buyer is asked to acknowledge the assignment of proceeds. A bank's charge for covering payment risk in this manner is borne by the seller.

13.3   UTILIZING PAYMENT UNDERTAKINGS AS A FOUNDATION FOR AN ALTERNATIVE FORM OF PAYMENT SECURITY

Payment undertakings have come to be used more generally, in the international arena, following a search for an alternative to the traditional forms of payment risk cover, because the traditional forms suffer from the following drawbacks.

13.3.1   Buyer's bank guarantees

- Buyers' banks tend to levy high charges for the opening of guarantees.
- Sometimes such guarantees have to be counter-guaranteed by a non-domestic bank, which raises an additional charge based on the financial standing of the opening bank, not on the financial standing of the buyer.
- Opening a guarantee utilizes an equivalent amount of the buyer's line of credit with its domestic bank, until the guarantee is drawn or expires. On the other hand, the buyer may be required to deposit cash collateral with the domestic bank, until the guarantee is drawn or expires.
- It is difficult for the buyer to arrange a partial bank guarantee in cases where the seller is prepared to carry a share of the payment risk in a single transaction.
- Guarantees opened by domestic banks do not allow non-domestic banks an opportunity to take direct risk in the name of the buyer.

13.3.2   Documentary credits (LCs)

- Buyers' banks tend to impose high charges for the opening of LCs.
- Sometimes such LCs have to be confirmed by a non-domestic bank, which raises an additional charge based on the financial standing of the opening bank, not on the financial standing of the buyer.
- Opening an LC utilizes an equivalent amount of the buyer's line of credit with its domestic bank, until the LC is drawn or expires. On the other hand, the buyer may be required to deposit cash collateral with the domestic bank, until the LC is drawn or expires.
- In cases where the seller is prepared to carry a share of the payment risk in a single transaction, it is difficult for the buyer to arrange a documentary LC to cover only part of a shipment.
- LCs opened by domestic banks do not allow non-domestic banks an opportunity to take direct risk in the name of the buyer.
- Processing LCs is an onerous administrative burden for the buyer.

13.3.3   Promissory notes

A promissory note (PN) creates an obligation entirely separate from the underlying purchase/sale contract. In order to create payment security before delivery, a PN based on an estimated quantity and an estimated due date must be obtained. This would enable a dishonest seller to demand payment even in the event that delivery did not take place. Therefore a significant element of trust is required on the part of the buyer.

13.3.4 On the other hand

The payment undertaking alternative attempts to overcome all these drawbacks by providing the following features:

- Unlimited unsecured credit terms for the buyer.
- No costs to the buyer for providing payment security.
- The buyer's traditional lines of credit are not restricted.
- Lower transaction costs achieved overall since "intermediary bank risk" related costs and "intermediary bank handling" fees are avoided. The savings can be shared by buyer and seller.
- Full flexibility for the seller to carry all or to share part of the buyer payment risk, transaction by transaction.
- A recognized and legally binding undertaking that is directly linked to a specific and identifiable contract.
- Only limited administration effort for the buyer. This alternative means a lot less work than either an LC or guarantee would mean for the buyer.
- Full flexibility for the seller to manage its country risk exposures independently of its buyer commercial risks. That is to say, if a buyer is thought to be creditworthy in respect of a particular transaction but the aggregate of transactions with other buyers in a particular country exceeds the seller's country limit, the excess risk can be covered without the need to involve the buyer. All the creditworthy buyers in the country in question continue to enjoy unsecured credit terms, while the seller is able to utilize the payment undertaking(s) of one or more buyer(s) to cover its excess country risk with a bank.

13.4 THE PAYMENT UNDERTAKING ALTERNATIVE PROCESS

Step 1

Buyer and seller negotiate and agree terms of a purchase/sale contract.

Step 2

The contract is signed. It includes the following clauses:

Credit: At least five days prior to delivery Buyer will send to Seller's bank, with a copy to Seller's financial contact, a Payment Undertaking in a format acceptable to Seller (bank details and payment undertaking text will be provided).

and

Assignment: This agreement will not be assignable by either party without the written consent of the other, which shall not be unreasonably withheld. However, in the event payment is not made by the Buyer on due date, Seller has the right to assign the financial rights under this agreement to a Bank without the prior consent of the Buyer.

Step 3

The seller decides how much of the commercial and/or country payment risk(s) to carry unsecured.

Step 4

The seller approaches several selected banks to obtain price and risk appetite indications, to cover – or share – the commercial and/or country payment risk(s).

Step 5

The seller chooses the best bank offer and asks the buyer to issue its payment undertaking to the chosen bank, using the text requested by the chosen bank. See Appendix 13.1 for an example of a payment undertaking text.

Step 6

If necessary the seller (representing the chosen bank) and buyer negotiate and agree the text of the payment undertaking.

Step 7

The buyer issues the payment undertaking and asks its own bank to authenticate its signatures and deliver the payment undertaking to the chosen bank, either in written form or by authenticated telex. The buyer's own bank would not normally charge for this service, since it takes no risk in simply confirming that the payment undertaking is signed by duly authorized officers of the buyer.

Step 8

The seller and chosen bank sign a risk participation agreement in terms of which the bank agrees to take over a portion of the commercial and/or country payment risk for a fee to be paid by the seller. See Appendix 13.2 for an example of a risk participation agreement.

Step 9

The goods are delivered under the terms of the purchase/sale contract.

Step 10

The seller sends an invoice and the required documents to the buyer, asking for payment to be made to the chosen bank, on the due date, for the seller's account.

Step 11

Payment is made on the agreed due date via the chosen bank and the transaction is closed.

13.5   NEGATIVE POINTS

The payment undertaking alternative requires the buyer to be involved in some additional administrative procedures, as listed:

- Firstly, in issuing the payment undertaking itself, and
- Secondly, in having the payment undertaking signatures authenticated by its own bank

13.6   POSITIVE POINTS

The seller can fully and flexibly use its line of credit for the buyer, to "average downwards" the cost of payment risk cover for each transaction. This is particularly relevant when the seller's risk appetite does not cover the full cost of a single transaction. Consider, for instance, the case where a seller has an approved credit line available of, say, $20 million for a buyer, but the value of a transaction is $40 million. Using the payment undertaking alternative the seller can simply ask a bank to cover only half of the payment risk, up to $20 million. The bank may charge, say, 1% per quarter to cover this risk. That would mean a transaction cost of only 0.5% per quarter ($20 million @ 1% divided by $40 million). This compares with an LC or guarantee covering the whole transaction, which would cost the full 1% per quarter on the whole transaction value.

The buyer's profile is raised among international banks when consideration is given at bank Credit Committee and Senior Executive level to the seller's request that the banks take on the commercial risk of the buyer directly.

The buyer's reputation is enhanced by building up a history of prompt payments with international banks.

The buyer has an option to approach participating banks later, that is, when it wants to extend its range of facilities beyond those available from domestic banks.

The buyer can share in the savings accruing from the reduced overall cost of payment risk cover.

13.7   SUMMARY

The payment undertaking alternative provides a firm foundation for establishing a long-term relationship between buyer and seller, a relationship which is free to expand regardless of the seller's need to manage its exposure to payment risk attaching to either the buyer or the buyer's country.

APPENDIX 13.1

PAYMENT UNDERTAKING FORMAT

QUOTE

Date: — *DATE* —

To: —*A-BANK*— —*A-COUNTRY*—
Telex Number: —*123456*— OR — *ADDRESS* —
Attention: —*MRS-ACCOUNT-MANAGER*—

Copy: —*YOUR COMPANY/THE SELLER*—
Telex Number: —*654321*— OR — *FAX NUMBER* —
Attention: —*MR-CREDIT-ANALYST*—

Message Number: —*3456XYZ78*—

SUBJECT: PAYMENT UNDERTAKING

We, —*ANOTHER-COMPANY*— (hereinafter called "—*ANOTHER*—" and/or "Buyer"), hereby confirm that we have agreed to purchase from —*YOUR-COMPANY*— (hereinafter called "Seller") approximately —*AGREED-AMOUNT*— of —*AGREED-GOODS*— at a price to be calculated as below for delivery commencing during —*AGREED-TIME-PERIOD*—.

The price calculation in —*AGREED-CURRENCY*— per —*AGREED-PRICE*— OR —*AGREED-PRICE-FORMULA*—.

Settlement of the price for delivery of —*AGREED-GOODS*— to —*AGREED-DESTI-NATION*— (to be finalised by —*AGREED-DATE*— in accordance with the contract).

All as per contract dated —*CONTRACT-DATE*— and subsequent amendments, if any.
Buyer Reference —*789012*—.
Seller Reference —*987654*—.

Subject to performance by the Seller, we —*ANOTHER*— hereby irrevocably and unconditionally confirm that we will pay the full invoice amount without any set-off, deduction or counter claim as designated in Seller's commercial invoice to the account of —*A-BANK*— at —*ANOTHER-BANK*— in —*AGREED-COUNTRY*— account number —*456789*—, on the due date per the contract being not later than — *AGREED-DAYS*— after the delivery date (delivery date equals day zero), against presentation of Seller's commercial invoice and the proof of delivery —(*BILL OF LADING FOR EXAMPLE*)—.

This undertaking is to be construed in accordance with English law with exclusive jurisdiction in the Courts of England.

Signed by:

Name: _____

Title: _____

Authorized Signatory for:

—*ANOTHER-COMPANY*—
—*ANOTHER-COUNTRY*—.

END QUOTE

APPENDIX 13.2

RISK PARTICIPATION AGREEMENT
EXAMPLE TEXT

SELLER
Address
City Country

'Seller' as Supplier

and

BANK
Address
City Country

'Bank' as Risk Participant

agree to assume part of the payment risk emanating from the following commercial transaction.

Sale

In accordance with contract...(reference number)...Seller has sold...(quantity)...of...(product description)...to be delivered in...(delivery month or date range)..., with payment due...(number)...days after...(Bill of Lading date or other reference date)...(the "Due Date") representing a total value of approximately USD..........

Purchase

...(full name of buyer)... ('Buyer') has purchased the above mentioned goods and has issued a Payment Undertaking.

Payment

The above mentioned amount of approximately USD............will be paid by Buyer directly to Bank's account with...(name of Bank's USD clearing bank)... on the Due Date (see above). These funds received on Bank's account will be remitted to Seller's account at...(name of Seller's bank)... net of Bank's fee, as per Paragraph 6 below, on the Due Date (see above).

Therefore, the parties agree as follows:

1. Risk Participation

Seller and Bank will share pro rata in the payment risk of Buyer on a several basis as follows:

a) Bank   USD . . . . (US Dollar . . . .)

b) Seller   USD . . . . (US Dollars . . . .)

2. Bank's Undertaking

Bank undertakes to purchase the pro rata share of the account receivable due and shall pay an amount up to its risk participation amount if and only if, Buyer fails to pay the contractual obligation on or before the 7th banking day in New York following the Due Date. Bank shall not have any obligation to make any payment to Seller if the failure by Buyer to pay is based upon non-performance by Seller – Bank accepts that it will be sufficient evidence of performance by Seller under the terms and conditions agreed between Buyer and Seller if Seller presents to Bank a copy of the . . . (Bill of Lading or other delivery document) . . . conforming to the terms and conditions agreed between Buyer and Seller in the underlying contract. In case of partial default by Buyer, Bank's purchase undertaking amount will be reduced to the pro rata share of its participation in the amount in default.

3. Seller's Undertaking

In case of a claim, Seller undertakes to sell and assign the pro rata share of the account receivable to Bank subject to the terms and conditions of this Risk Participation Agreement.

Seller is responsible to obtain all necessary legal and other approvals required for Seller to enter into this agreement.

4. Effective Date

This purchase undertaking will be effective and legally binding on the date Bank receives this Agreement, duly countersigned by Seller, and all Conditions Precedent have been satisfied.

5. Duration

This agreement is valid until . . . (date) . . . Any claims hereunder must be received by Bank no later than . . . (date) . . . . Notwithstanding the foregoing, this agreement shall not expire as to any claims made prior to . . . (date) . . . which have not been finally settled between Bank and Seller prior to . . . (date) . . .

6. Pricing

Seller agrees to pay to Bank ... (agreed charge rate) ... on Bank's aggregate maximum risk participation of USD .... (US Dollars ....). This commission will be deducted from the payments received, or in case of non-payment by Buyer, by direct payment arranged by Seller to Bank.

7. Conditions Precedent

In order for this Agreement to become effective Seller will provide Bank with the following documents:

(a) Copy/ies of the related commercial invoice(s).
(b) A payment undertaking signed by Buyer (as per enclosure text). Buyer's signature is to be authenticated by a well known commercial bank in form and substance satisfactory to Bank.
(c) Copy/ies of appropriate shipping documents.

8. Conditions for Claim

Bank shall purchase, from Seller, Buyer's account receivable pursuant to this agreement and shall pay the respective amount to Seller within two banking days in New York after the presentation of the following documents to Bank:

(i) Copy of Seller's telex or facsimile sent to Buyer protesting non-receipt of funds on Due Date ('Protest Notice');
(ii) Not earlier than four banking days in New York after submitting the Protest Notice, Seller's statement as follows:

Seller hereby claims under the unfunded Risk Participation Agreement dated ... (date) ... and signed by Seller and Bank, and certifies to Bank that full/Partial Payment ... (as applicable) ... of USD .... has not been received by Seller and that Seller requests Bank to honour this request for purchase of Buyer's account receivable in the pro rata amount of USD .... Seller confirms that this non-receipt of payment has not arisen out of any breach of contract by Seller under Seller's contract with Buyer, and Seller's rights which are to be assigned to Bank are free and clear of withholdings, counterclaims, and setoffs.

Provided:

(a) Seller will not have agreed to any alterations to the financial terms of its contract with Buyer without Bank's prior consent.
(b) Seller shall disclose and assign the respective claim to Bank and agrees to furnish to Bank promptly upon Bank's request such documentation and perform such reasonable legal acts as Bank in its sole determination, deems necessary or advisable to constitute or perfect Bank's claim on Buyer in the event Buyer fails to pay under its payment undertaking and Bank has made payment to Seller pursuant to its undertaking described herein.

(c) In addition Seller agrees to cooperate fully with Bank in any legal or other proceedings brought by Bank against Buyer.

All costs and expenses (excluding in-house legal or administrative expense) incurred by Bank in connection with the collection of any amounts payable by Buyer, in connection with the enforcement of any document relating to the payment undertaking, shall be borne between Bank and Seller pro rata on the basis of this Risk Participation Agreement.

9. Notices

Any notice under this Agreement shall be in writing (including telegraphic, telex or facsimile communication). All such notices shall be deemed to be given when transmitted by telex and the appropriate answer-back is received, transmitted by facsimile machine and confirmed in writing, delivered to the telegraphic office, personally delivered or, in the case of a mailed notice, when sent by registered or certified mail, postage prepaid to the participants" above-mentioned addresses or to such other address as may be advised from time to time to Bank in writing.

10. Governing Law and Jurisdiction

This Agreement shall be governed by and construed in accordance with the law of England. All legal aspects of the relationship between Seller and Bank shall be governed by English Law and the place of exclusive jurisdiction of lawsuits and any other kinds of legal proceedings shall be the Courts of England.

....

Agreed accepted by

SELLER

Dated:.................

....

Agreed accepted by

BANK

Dated:...............

14

Trade Credit Risk ScoreCard and Limit Model

14.1 INTRODUCTION

A practical example of a Trade Credit Risk ScoreCard is presented in this chapter to illustrate this alternative or supplemental approach to corporate customer credit analysis. This technique uses the Balanced ScoreCard concept to create scoring models that require analysts to give due weight to non-financial factors when assessing credit risk. A ScoreCard provides a logical and standardized framework for analysts to use when working through the examination of a customer's position, before making a credit decision.

The objectives of developing a ScoreCard and integrated limit model are to:

- Make credit limit decisions in a standardized and systematic way, based on facts
- Make credit decisions which align with and support your company strategy
- Speed up credit decisions and enable the use of technology to a greater extent

The ScoreCard produces an overall risk score based on simple weighting, with some easy-to-understand algebraic adjustments. It has been designed to ensure discrimination between various grades of risk in a transparent fashion.

In addition the ScoreCard has been enhanced to provide internal credit risk ratings. Trade credit risk ratings are useful in terms of receivable portfolio analysis, and in establishing whether your company is adequately compensated for the risk carried when advancing trade credit.

The core tenet of a ScoreCard is to *imitate* the thought processes of a team of highly experienced and qualified credit analysts, and thereby – on each occasion the ScoreCard is used – to reach the same conclusion that such a group of experts would have reached, using traditional methods. The method adopted is often referred to as "rules based" scoring.

In order to develop a useful ScoreCard the designer has to take into account the requirements and peculiarities of your company, as well as those of your potential market. A ScoreCard should be tested as extensively as possible before it is utilized. Subjective elements must be reviewed regularly, to ensure that the model maintains its accuracy.

The ScoreCard does not eliminate the need for diligent analysis of the facts, it merely standardizes the process and enables the production of a useful numeric score. In order for an analyst to complete the ScoreCard proficiently it will always be necessary to research the customer, or potential customer, being graded. This will become clear as the questions are reviewed.

The particular questions used in this exercise were chosen using the following criteria:

- A question must (as far as possible) be capable of being answered by reference to objective information. In other words everyone in possession of the relevant facts should choose the same answer to the question.
- Only the most significant questions should be utilized. The list should be strictly limited in order to ensure that each answer, one way or the other, actually influences the overall score. If too many questions are included in a ScoreCard, each question has very little impact on the final outcome. In fact many answers cancel each other out, leading to production of a mediocre score that is essentially useless for the purpose. The purpose is to provide a clear and understandable basis on which to make a decision.
- The questions should adequately represent all aspects considered important in making a decision. They should provide the necessary balance to ensure that consideration of financial information reporting past performance does not smother consideration of non-numeric factors. The latter have been proved time and again to be the more likely cause of difficulties, incompetent or dishonest management being the most obvious perils not apparent from a usual financial analysis.
- Questions should attempt to replicate the thought processes of highly experienced analysts, in order to produce standardized results of premium quality.

14.2   A TRADE CREDIT RISK SCORECARD

The ScoreCard example provided here can be set up on a spreadsheet, without the need to use any complex programming skills. This Trade Credit Risk ScoreCard consists of a series of questions arranged in four sections, namely "financial information", "management ability and integrity", "market risk", and "country risk". Certain alternative answers are possible for each question. Each answer has a score associated. These raw scores are weighted and adjusted, using simple formulas, to produce a trade credit score that feeds into a limit model.

Recognizing that it is more often than not impossible to obtain the usual financial statements for potential customers, and for many existing customers, the first section is provided in two alternative versions. Section One A is to be used when financial statements (income statement, balance sheet, cash flow statement and explanatory notes) are available. Section One B is to be used when financial statements are not available.

Section One A: Financial information

QA1: What is the financial analysis summary score?   100

Enter the score related to your assessment of the customer's financial strength, scored as shown in Table 14.1. Example "financial strength excellent" equals score of 100.

QA2: Is the audit report clean (unqualified)? Yes = 10; No or financials not audited = 0   10

In this example answer "yes" equals score of 10.

QA3: How recent is the financial information? <6 months old = 10; <1 year old = 6;   10
<18 months old = 2; older = 0

The older the available annual report, the lower the score. Example financial information less than six months old equals score of 10.

QA4: What is the customer's equity at risk? >twice the proposed limit = 20; >equal   20
to = 10; >half = 5; less = 0

The rationale for this question is that the more the "owners" of the customer have to lose the more likely they are to work hard to ensure the company remains successful. Example: net tangible equity is more than twice the limit you propose to advance (put at risk) equals a score of 20.

QA5: What is the customer's defensive interval? >32 days = 20: >16 days = 16; >8   20
days = 10; >4 days = 4; less = 0

In this example the customer's defensive interval[1] is greater than 32 days equals a score of 20.

QA6: Was cash flow from operations minus dividends positive? Yes = 20; No = 0   20

This question examines whether the owners took less cash out of the business than it generated through normal operations. Example: "yes" equals 20.

QA7: What is the "days payables outstanding" number equal to? Normal terms = 20;   20
less than 150% of normal = 10: more = 0

If normal terms are "30 days" and "days payables outstanding"[2] is 30 or less, score 20; if it is 45 or less score 10; if more score 0.

One A: Subsection score (actual/converted)   200   0.50

The actual subsection score – called X in the formula – is converted as follows:

$$Xc = 20/(X/5)$$

Ultimately this ScoreCard will produce a credit risk score ranging from 0.50 (lowest risk of default) upward, with a score of more than 5 indicating an unacceptably high risk of default.

[1] A customer's "defensive interval" is the time (expressed in "days") during which the customer can continue to operate its business utilizing only cash resources (liquid assets) actually on hand on the relevant balance sheet date.

$$\text{Defensive Interval} = \text{Quick Assets}/\text{Daily Cash Operating Expenses}$$
$$\text{Daily Cash Operating Expenses} = (\text{Sales} + \text{or} - (\text{A/R this year} - \text{A/R last year})$$
$$- \text{Operation's Cash Flow})/365$$

(A/R = Accounts Receivable.) The number calculated for the "defensive interval" indicates how many days the "defensive assets" can continue to support normal operations despite a complete cessation of revenues. The "revenue cessation" concept provides a base measure against which to assess the financial reserves available to a company. It makes possible the direct comparison of a company with its competitor or peer companies.

[2] A *days payables outstanding* number is usually calculated as follows:

$$\text{Accounts Payable}/(\text{Cost of Sales}/365)$$

Table 14.1   Financial strength assessment

	Summary	Score
Customer's financial strength is judged to be	Excellent	100
	Good	80
	Above average	60
	Average	40
	Marginal	20
	Poor	0

The ScoreCard user should undertake an analysis of the customer's financial statements using available tools. After completing the analysis the results should be reviewed and the customer's financial strength assessed by ranking against its peer (competitor) companies, using the scale provided.

This can be accomplished by utilizing the DecisionDesktop financial analysis tools provided by eCredit.com Inc. (http://www.ecredit.com), for example.

Section One B: Financial information

QB1: Are financial statements available? No $=0$	0

Your company is considering investing in the business activity of your customer, by providing working capital through supplier credit. The lack of transparency evidenced by the withholding of financial information must be factored into the credit risk score calculation. This is achieved by recording zero points here.

QB2: How many days late is the customer reported to pay creditors? $<5=30$; $<30=10$; more $=0$	30

This information should be obtained from credit reference agencies and direct from other creditors. Credit discussion groups including your competitors will be useful. Also direct approaches to logically deduced suppliers who are not competitors. Do not rely solely on references supplied by the customer. Example of suppliers paid within 5 days of due date scores 30.

QB3: Has any one of the owners or executives been involved in a failed business? No $=10$; Yes $=0$	10

Take the answer as "no" for this example, scores 10.

QB4: Is there evidence of extravagant expenditure (spending out of line with normal expected income levels in their business) either within the business or by executives in their private capacity? No $=30$; Yes $=0$	30

A "yes" answer would indicate that the owners/executives are using creditors' money (supplier credit) to finance their lifestyles and/or are poor financial managers. Either case would be a serious warning sign. In this example take the answer to be "no", scores 30.

QB5: Does the customer have an active account with a well-respected bank that is active in the appropriate market? Yes $=5$; No $=0$	5

A respected bank will undertake due diligence when accepting a customer. Operating an active account with such a bank is a positive indicator. In this example answer "yes", score 5.

QB6: Is customer's legal counsel a reputable firm? Yes $=5$; No $=0$	5

A respected legal firm will undertake due diligence when accepting a customer. In this example answer "yes", score 5.

QB7: Have any key employees resigned in the past three months? No $=20$; Yes $=0$	20

Resignations may indicate that such "insiders" either disagreed with the business ethics of the leaders, or were concerned they may not be paid, or saw no long-term future with the company. Example: answer "no" scores 20.

One B: Subsection score (actual/converted)	100	1.00

The actual subsection score – called X in the formula – is converted as follows:

$$Xc = 20/(X/5).$$

Section Two: Management ability and integrity

Q8: How many years has the company been in business? >15 years = 20; >7 years = 10; less = 0	20

If it is accepted that economic cycles repeat every seven years, a company that has survived in business through at least two cycles has proved the necessary organizational resilience. Example of company in business for more than 15 years equals a score of 20.

Q9: How are CEO and CFO appointed? on merit = 20; one or both "political" or "family" appointments = 0	20

Political appointees are likely to make decisions based on political considerations rather than "best business", and family appointees may be weak and/or unsuitable leaders. Example answer of "both on merit" equals score of 20.

Q10: Has there been any scandal in the past two years? No = 10; Yes = 0. Has there been any "dispute" with the authorities in the last two years? No = 10; Yes = 0	20

This is an attempt to factor into the score management integrity. The argument is that if management lack integrity this will be signalled by the occurrence of disputes (e.g. alleged failure to remit duties collected) or scandals (e.g. employees injured due to unsafe conditions). The question requires a "no" or "yes" answer to each question. No = 10 but Yes = 0. There is no provision for a company with just a little scandal to earn some points, any scandal equals zero points. The objective is to elicit an answer that makes a difference to the overall result, even after it is mingled with the other answers. In this example accept there was no scandal and no dispute, hence a score of 10 + 10.

Q11: Was at least one executive a senior government official or minister or is one a political appointee? Yes = 10; No = 0	10

The theory is that the executive's understanding of the bureaucratic processes or government network will enable the company to avoid regulatory difficulties and obtain any necessary permissions. Example: score 10.

Q12: Is there evidence of an effective strategic response to market and/or competitive forces in the last three years? Yes = 30; No = 0	30

If, after reviewing all the information available, the analyst is able to point to one strategic decision by the executive that has been or is likely to be effective, the points should be awarded. Absence of strategic initiatives or existence of only failed or ineffective strategic initiatives scores zero. Example: score 30.

Subsection score (actual/converted)	100	1.00

The actual subsection score – called Y in the formula – is converted as follows:

$$Yc = 20/(Y/5)$$

Section Three: Market risk

Q13: Are your competitors offering or providing unsecured credit to the customer? Yes = 50; No = 0   50

This question produces a good proxy for a credit reference and also addresses the competitive issue related to credit. Often sellers adopt a less risk-averse stance when necessary to match their competition in respect of credit terms. The result must be 50 points or zero. In this example score 50.

Q14: Does your company wish to increase its market share? Yes = 20; No = 0   20

Sellers use credit terms as a tool to assist efforts to increase market share in many instances. This motivation is therefore often considered an important aspect of credit risk assessment. Score 20 in this example.

Q15: What is your potential sustainable profit margin on sales to this customer? High = 50; Medium = 20; Low = 0   50

In commercial situations it is understood that "higher profit often means higher risk". Hence the potential to earn a sustainable high profit margin, for a reasonable period, is often accepted as a valid reason to tolerate higher payment risk. Score 50 in this example.

Q16: Is this customer a potential buyer of "no-value-goods" or "high-retention-cost" goods? Yes = 40; No = 0   40

These are two more valid commercial reasons to accept higher payment risk. "No-value-goods" would usually be by-products that will attract disposal costs if not sold on credit. "High-retention-cost" goods incur high storage costs if not sold on credit. Score 40 in this example.

Q17: Is this customer operating in a regional market that is depressed, without having any counteracting exposure? No = 20; Yes = 0   20

Despite the best efforts of a customer, if its sole or main market is depressed, its associated default risk will increase. This is so unless it is able to shift the focus of its business to an alternative market, at a relatively low cost. The term "market" refers to the general economic conditions prevailing. Score 20 for a "no" answer in this example.

Q18: Is this customer operating in a type of trade that is depressed, without having any counteracting exposure? No = 20; Yes = 0   20

As with the previous comment, if a customer's sole or main type of trade is depressed, its associated default risk will increase. This is so unless it is able to shift the focus of its business to an alternative, at a relatively low cost. The term 'type of trade" refers here to the business sector relevant to your customer's principal commercial activity. Score 20 for a "no" answer in this example.

Subsection score (actual/converted)	200	1.00

The actual sub-section score – called Z in the formula – is converted as follows:

$$Zc = 20/(Z/10)$$

Section Four: Country risk

Q19: Is this customer based in an OECD member country: Yes = 100 (and other questions in this section = 0); No = 0	100	

If this customer is based in an OECD[3] member country, enter a score of 100 and this section will be complete. However, if it is not, enter zero and answer the next two questions, i.e. Q20 and Q21. *If you are not exporting goods or services* (if the customer is based in your country), answer "yes" to this question even if your country is not a member of the OECD. For this example answer "yes" equals a score of 100.

Q20: What is the FitchRatings' long-term foreign currency sovereign rating? AAA/AA = 60; A/BBB = 50; BB = 40; B = 30; CCC = 20; CC = 10; C/D = 0	0	

These ratings are stipulated because they are available on the FitchRatings website (http://www.fitchibca.com).

Q21: What is the host country production of the product you are exporting as a percentage of host country consumption? <25% = 40; <50% = 30; <75% = 20; More = 0	0	

It is suggested that "country risk" is reduced to the extent that the product that you are exporting cannot be substituted by local production, in the host country. Relevant statistics are usually available from the websites of international non-government agencies such as the International Monetary Fund or the World Bank.

Subsection score (actual/converted)	100	1.00

The actual subsection score – called R in the formula – is converted as follows:

$$Rc = 20/(R/5)$$

[3] OECD – the Organization for Economic Cooperation and Development (http://www.oecd.org) had 30 member countries as of the first quarter of 2003, as follows: Australia, Austria, Belgium, Canada, Czech Republic, Denmark, Finland, France, Germany, Greece, Hungary, Iceland, Ireland, Italy, Japan, Korea, Luxembourg, Mexico, Netherlands, New Zealand, Norway, Poland, Portugal, Slovak Republic, Spain, Sweden, Switzerland, Turkey, United Kingdom, United States.

Section Five: Selected score exaggerator

Add together the scores from QA1 (or QB2 and QB4), Q12, Q13, Q17, Q18   320
and the Section Four total then enter the sum here

In this example, add QA1 = 100 plus Q12 = 30 plus Q13 = 50 plus Q17 = 20 plus Q18 = 20 plus Section Four = 100, making a sum total of 320.

The original ScoreCard failed to sufficiently discriminate between low-risk, medium-risk and high-risk companies. This section was added in order to correct that flaw. The six (or seven) items selected here are considered to be those that would each be a potential "roadblock" in the minds of experienced credit analysts. Therefore each such factor carries more weight if it is negative than it does if it is positive.

Subsection score (actual/converted)   320   5.00

The actual subsection score – called E in the formula – is converted as follows:

$$Ec = (320/E)^*(5^*((320/E)^3))$$

The effect of this formula is to increase the subsection converted score exponentially, if the actual score (the sum of the six/seven chosen individual scores) decreases. This effectively increases the overall score – indicating higher risk of default – thus discriminating between good, indifferent and bad companies.

Overall trade credit risk score   **0.50**

The overall trade risk score is calculated by adding together the five converted scores and dividing that total by 17. The formula is $= (Xc + Yc + Zc + Rc + Ec)/17$.

The denominator was arrived at simply as the number required to produce the target minimum possible score of 0.5.

14.3   A TRADE CREDIT LIMIT MODEL AND INTERNAL RATING SCHEME

This trade credit exposure limit model complements the Trade Credit Risk ScoreCard described in the previous section. The overall trade credit risk score produced by the ScoreCard is used to calculate one element of the model, and can be used to produce an internal credit rating. The latter will be useful in terms of portfolio analysis and portfolio risk management, in relation to trade credit exposure.

14.3.1   Rules of the trade credit limit model

The model consists of four restrictive parameters:

1. The limit must not exceed a certain prescribed proportion of your company's equity – say 10% – in order to regulate concentration risk.
2. The limit must not exceed the amount necessary to accommodate normal business requirements. This amount can be forecast in consultation with marketing colleagues, based on planned activity.
3. The limit must not exceed the amount calculated according to the formula: *(company's cost of sales) multiplied by ((1/(the trade Risk Score))*0.05)*. This formula effectively scales down the potential limit as the score indicates increasing risk of

default. It also ensures that any limit will be suitably adjusted automatically, whenever the ScoreCard is updated with fresh information.
4. The limit is to be set at *Zero* if the trade credit risk score exceeds 4.49, indicating a rating of CCC+ or worse.

14.3.2   Credit limit model considerations

Many credit analysts consider that a credit limit should not exceed a fixed percentage of a company's net tangible equity (NTE). A commonly used limit factor is 5% of NTE. The temptation in using this methodology is to do little analysis beyond calculating 5% of NTE. This practice is too simplistic and can lead analysts to avoid taking responsibility for making a decision. It is too easy to simply "blame" the formula, rather than to engage mental power and think through a limit decision.

NTE is not an ideal basis on which to calculate a credit limit. It may indicate a customer's "safety net" in the event that it has difficulties, a "safety net" that could be used to settle its debts. However, its value depends heavily on the value of the customer's assets, a value that notoriously tends to diminish very rapidly if a company falters. The main contra indicator regarding the use of NTE is that it bears no relation to cash flow or liquidity. Yet payment and day-to-day operations rely exclusively on cash flow and liquidity.

Moreover, a formula that requires the application of a simplistic percentage to NTE is of no use if the NTE figure is not known. In other words, when financial statements are not available, you are unable to determine a credit limit based on NTE.

14.3.3   Commercial usage

In practice a credit limit is often calculated based on the analyst's estimate (after questioning the sales manager and the customer) of the:

- Quantities to be delivered under each invoice (multiplied by)
- Price (multiplied by)
- Maximum number of deliveries that will be outstanding (not yet paid for) at any one time

The "maximum number of deliveries that will be outstanding (not yet paid for) at any one time" is determined by estimating the "cash flow cycle"; that is, the "days inventory (from order date to sale date)" plus the "days sales outstanding" minus the "credit terms offered". The number of deliveries outstanding will equal the number of orders initiated during one cash flow cycle.

An analyst then considers whether the customer will (a) be able to meet the invoices when they fall due, and (b) qualify for the credit limit calculated.

14.3.4   Relating the maximum credit level to cost of sales

Considering the practical commercial approach outlined above, a credit limit calculation based on the customer's estimated "cost of sales" during the next 12 months would seem more appropriate. In the case of companies that provide sales forecasts this figure (or preferably the figure applicable to your sector) could be estimated based on previously reported gross profit levels.

On the other hand, when financial statements and forecasts are not available, or for new companies, it should be possible to estimate "cost of sales" by working with sales colleagues to estimate the quantity of goods the customer should sell over the next 12 months. At the very least you could estimate the market for the goods you sell and your customer's market share, hence your customer's potential sales quantity. This quantity multiplied by your forecast average sales price would yield an estimated cost of sales.

An annual cost of sales figure divided by 365 days, and multiplied by the normal industry credit term, will yield the maximum trade-related "accounts payable" that your customer should have outstanding at any one time. If you were to supply 100% of the customer's needs, you would have to offer a credit limit equal to 100% of the forecast trade payables amount.

Given this information (albeit an estimate) you can construct a formula starting with a willingness (according to your risk appetite – particularly your appetite for concentration risk) to grant, say, a limit equal to 10% of an AAA rated customer's annual cost of goods sold. This 10% example figure is based on 80% of 45 days of "payables" outstanding at any one time. This allows for some overlapping of transactions when normal terms are 30 days after date of delivery. The calculation is:

$$80\% * (45/365) = 10\%$$

Your formula should create reducing percentages, to apply to the "cost of goods sold", as the credit rating or trade credit score indicates increasing risk of default.

The next step would be to test your formula with some examples to determine if it produces reasonable limits, and to adjust it if necessary.

The attraction of this method is that the limit model can be applied fairly easily to customers that do not provide financial information, and perfectly easily to those that do provide information. It is also based on the customer's needs and can be related to the amount of potential business available from the customer. You can then regulate your ambition to gain a share of that business according to your perception of the credit risk. Alternatively you can solicit more business only if you are prepared to incur the additional cost of obtaining payment risk security. A credit limit determined on this basis could double as a sales target.

Relating credit limits to "cost of sales" is far superior to working with a simplistic 5% of NTE. In effect, in terms of the latter approach, a credit analyst mechanistically limits your sales potential.

14.3.5 Internal trade credit rating conversion chart and maximum limit indicator

Suggested credit rating equivalents, in relation to various overall trade credit risk scores produced by the ScoreCard, are shown in Table 14.2. Also shown are maximum credit limit indicators as percentages of "cost of sales", in ranges related directly to the credit ratings.

Table 14.2

Score	Rating	Credit limit as % of cost of sales*
0.50–0.74	AAA	10.00–6.76
0.75–0.99	AA+	6.67–5.05
1.00–1.24	AA	5.00–4.03
1.25–1.49	AA–	4.00–3.36
1.50–1.74	A+	3.33–2.87
1.75–1.99	A	2.86–2.51
2.00–2.24	A–	2.50–2.23
2.25–2.49	BBB+	2.22–2.01
2.50–2.74	BBB	2.00–1.82
2.75–2.99	BBB–	1.82–1.67
3.00–3.24	BB+	1.67–1.54
3.25–3.49	BB	1.54–1.43
3.50–3.74	BB–	1.43–1.34
3.75–3.99	B+	1.33–1.25
4.00–4.24	B	1.25–1.18
4.25–4.49	B–	1.18–1.11
4.50–4.74	CCC+	Zero
4.75–4.99	CCC	Zero
5.00–5.25	CCC–	Zero
Higher	D	Zero

* The proportion to be applied to the cost of sales amount, in order to determine the maximum trade credit limit, is calculated as follows:

((1) divided by (the Trade Credit Risk Score))

then multiplied by (0.05)

Appendices
Credit ScoreCard Analysis Examples

I Bank A – Subsidiary of an International Bank

Bank A 1999 financials ($ millions)

Net income	14.60
Total assets	182.71
Liabilities	145.13
Net tangible equity	*37.58*

Section One: Bank rating and financial information

Q1:	What is the bank rating agency score?	0	
Q2:	How recent is the financial information? <6 months old = 20; <1 year old = 10; <18 months old = 5; older = 0	20	
Q3:	What is the bank's equity? >10% of the proposed limit = 80; >8% = 60; >6% = 40; less = 0	80	
	Subsection score (actual/converted)	100	3.00

Table: Score per bank rating

Standard and Poor's	Moody's	Fitch	Score
Not rated	Not rated	Not rated	0

Section Two: Management ability and integrity

Q4: How many years has bank been in business? >15 years = 20; >7 years = 10; less = 0	0
Q5: Is the bank managed by officers of a significant transnational financial services group, under management contract? Yes = 20; No = 0	20
Q6: Has there been any scandal in the past two years? No = 20; Yes = 0. Has there been any "dispute" with the authorities in the last two years? No = 20; Yes = 0	40
Q7: Is the bank a member of a significant transnational financial services group (meaning >50% owned)? Yes = 80; No = 0	80
Q8: Does the bank carry the name of a significant transnational financial services group? Yes = 40; No = 0	40

Subsection score (actual/converted)	180	1.11

Section Three: Relationship with your company

Q9: Does your company have an active relationship with this bank or the related bank group? Yes = 50; No = 0	50

Subsection score (actual/converted)	50	1.00

Section Four: Country risk

Q10: Is the bank based in an OECD member country? Yes = 100 (and other questions in this section = 0); No = 0	0
Q11: What is the FitchRatings' long-term foreign currency sovereign rating? AAA/AA = 60; A/BBB = 50; BB = 40; B = 30; CCC = 20; CC = 10; C/D = 0	30
Q12: What is the host country production of the product you are exporting, as a percentage of host country consumption? <25% = 40; <50% = 30; <75% = 20; more = 0	0

Subsection score (actual/converted)	30	3.33

Section Five: Selected score exaggerator

Add together the scores from Q1, Q3, Q6, Q7 and the Section Four total then enter the sum here	230

Subsection score (actual/converted)	230	51.37

Overall bank risk score	*3.32*
Internal bank rating	*BB*
Maximum exposure limit indicated ($ millions)	*11.31*

II BANK B – LOCAL BANK IN AN EMERGING MARKET COUNTRY

Bank B 1999 financials ($ millions)

Net income	21.67
Total assets	585.50
Liabilities	490.49
Net tangible equity	*95.01*

Section One: Bank rating and financial information

Q1: What is the bank rating agency score?   60

Q2: How recent is the financial information? <6 months old = 20; <1 year old = 10; <18 months old = 5; older = 0   20

Q3: What is the bank's equity? >10% of the proposed limit = 80; >8% = 60; >6% = 40; less = 0   80

Subsection score (actual/converted)   160   1.88

Table: Score per bank rating

Standard and Poor's	Moody's	Fitch	Score
B	–	B	60

Section Two: Management ability and integrity

Q4: How many years has bank been in business? >15 years = 20; >7 years = 10; less = 0   0

Q5: Is the bank managed by officers of a significant transnational financial services group, under management contract? Yes = 20; No = 0   0

Q6: Has there been any scandal in the past two years? No = 20; Yes = 0. Has there been any "dispute" with the authorities in the last two years? No = 20; Yes = 0   40

Q7: Is the bank a member of a significant transnational financial services group (meaning >50% owned) Yes = 80; No = 0   0

Q8: Does the bank carry the name of a significant transnational financial services group? Yes = 40; No = 0   0

Subsection score (actual/converted)   40   5.00

Section Three: Relationship with your company

Q9: Does your company have an active relationship with this bank or the related bank group? Yes $= 50$; No $= 0$	50	
Subsection score (actual/converted)	50	1.00

Section Four: Country risk

Q10: Is the bank based in an OECD member country? Yes $= 100$ (and other questions in this section $= 0$); No $= 0$	0	
Q11: What is the FitchRatings' long-term foreign currency sovereign rating? AAA/AA $= 60$; A/BBB $= 50$; BB $= 40$; B $= 30$; CCC $= 20$; CC $= 10$; C/D $= 0$	30	
Q12: What is the host country production of the product you are exporting, as a percentage of host country consumption? $<25\% = 40$; $<50\% = 30$; $<75\% = 20$; more $= 0$	0	
Subsection score (actual/converted)	30	3.33

Section Five: Selected score exaggerator

Add together the scores from Q1, Q3, Q6, Q7 and the Section Four total then enter the sum here	210	
Subsection score (actual/converted)	210	67.49
Overall bank risk score		*4.37*
Internal bank rating		*B−*
Maximum exposure limit indicated ($ millions)		*21.73*

III   COMPANY A

DuPont[1] analysis Company A 1998 financials ($ millions)

Sales	907.01	
Cost of goods sold	793.93	
Other expenses (excluding interest)	28.95	
Return on sales before interest		9.28%
Net interest paid	18.91	
Return on sales after interest		7.19%
Assets		
Other current (including cash)	226.43	
Accounts receivable	92.89	
Inventory	58.09	
Fixed assets	227.24	
Asset turnover		150.01%
Liabilities		
Accounts payable	54.66	
Overdraft/notes payable	7.28	
Other current	66.95	
Long term	16.93	
Net tangible equity	458.83	
Leverage		131.78%
Return on equity		18.34%
Return on equity after interest		14.21%
Defensive interval	9.47 days	

[1] DuPont analysis – a system of analysis that focuses on the interrelationships between "net profit/sales" (net profit margin), "sales/total assets" (total asset turnover), and "total assets/net tangible equity" (financial leverage or gearing). Any decision or action that affects one or more of these three aspects of a business will affect "return on equity". The basic DuPont formula is

(net profit/sales) * (sales/total assets) * (total assets/net tangible equity)

= return on equity (also termed ROCE – return on capital employed)

Section One A: Financial information

QA1: What is the financial analysis summary score?	40
QA2: Is the audit report clean (unqualified)? Yes = 10; no or financials not audited = 0	10
QA3: How recent is the financial information? <6 months old = 10; <1 year old = 6; <18 months old = 2; older = 0	2
QA4: What is the customer's equity at risk? >twice the proposed limit = 20; >equal to = 10; >half = 5; less = 0	20
QA5: What is the customer's defensive interval? >32 days = 20; >16 days = 16; >8 days = 10; >4 days = 4; less = 0	10
QA6: Was cash flow from operations minus dividends positive ? Yes = 20; No = 0	20
QA7: What is the "days payables outstanding" number equal to? Normal terms = 20; less than 150% of normal = 10; more = 0	10

One A: Subsection score (actual/converted)	112	0.89

Table: Financial strength assessment

	Summary	Score
Customer's financial strength is judged to be	Average	40

Section Two: Management ability and integrity

Q8: How many years has the company been in business? >15 years = 20; >7 years = 10; less = 0	0
Q9: How are CEO and CFO appointed? On merit = 20; one or both "political" or "family" appointments = 0	0
Q10: Has there been any scandal in the past two years? No = 10; Yes = 0. Has there been any "dispute" with the authorities in the last two years? No = 10; Yes = 0	20
Q11: Was at least one executive a senior government official or minister or is one a political appointee? Yes = 10; No = 0	10
Q12: Is there evidence of an effective strategic response to market and/or competitive forces in the last three years? Yes = 30; No = 0	30

Subsection score (actual/converted)	60	1.67

Section Three: Market risk

Q13: Are your competitors offering or providing unsecured credit to the customer? Yes = 50; No = 0	50	
Q14: Does your company wish to increase its market share? Yes = 20; No = 0	0	
Q15: What is your potential sustainable profit margin on sales to this customer? High = 50; Medium = 20; Low = 0	0	
Q16: Is this customer a potential buyer of 'no-value-goods" or "high-retention-cost" goods? Yes = 40; No = 0	0	
Q17: Is this customer operating in a regional market that is depressed, without having any counteracting exposure? No = 20; Yes = 0	0	
Q18: Is this customer operating in a type of trade that is depressed, without having any counteracting exposure? No = 20; Yes = 0	0	
Subsection score (actual/converted)	50	4.00

Section Four: Country risk

Q19: Is this customer based in an OECD member country? Yes = 100 (and other questions in this section = 0); No = 0	100	
Q20: What is the FitchRatings' long-term foreign currency sovereign rating? AAA/AA = 60; A/BBB = 50; BB = 40; B = 30; CCC = 20; CC = 10; C/D = 0	0	
Q21: What is the host country production of the product you are exporting, as a percentage of host country consumption? <25% = 40; <50% = 30; <75% = 20; more = 0	0	
Subsection score (actual/converted)	100	1.00

Section Five: Selected score exaggerator

Add together the scores from QA1, Q12, Q13, Q17, Q18 and the Section Four total then enter the sum here	220	
Subsection score (actual/converted)	220	22.38
Overall trade credit risk score		*1.76*
Trade credit rating		*A*
Maximum trade credit limit indication ($ millions)		*22.54*

IV   COMPANY B

DuPont analysis Company B 1999 financials ($ millions)

Sales	968.65	
Cost of goods sold	839.39	
Other expenses (excluding interest)	75.66	
Return on sales before interest		5.53%
Net interest paid	14.60	
Return on sales after interest		4.03%
Assets		
Other current (including cash)	72.82	
Accounts receivable	115.34	
Inventory	123.87	
Fixed assets	184.14	
Asset turnover		195.22%
Liabilities		
Accounts payable	82.54	
Overdraft/notes payable	211.18	
Other current	124.71	
Long term	16.29	
Net tangible equity	61.46	
Leverage		807.29%
Return on equity		87.21%
Return on equity after interest		63.46%
Defensive interval	0.86 days	

Section One A: Financial information

QA1: What is the financial analysis summary score?	20
QA2: Is the audit report clean (unqualified)? Yes = 10; No or financials not audited = 0	0
QA3: How recent is the financial information? <6 months old = 10; <1 year old = 6; <18 months old = 2; older = 0	6
QA4: What is the customer's equity at risk? >twice the proposed limit = 20; >equal to = 10; >half = 5; less = 0	20
QA5: What is the customer's defensive interval? >32 days = 20; >16 days = 16; >8 days = 10; >4 days = 4; less = 0	0
QA6: Was cash flow from operations minus dividends positive ? Yes = 20; No = 0	20
QA7: What is the "days payables outstanding" number equal to? Normal terms = 20; less than 150% of Normal = 10; more = 0	20

One A: Subsection score (actual/converted)	86	1.16

Table: Financial strength assessment

	Summary	Score
Customer's financial strength is judged to be	Marginal	20

Section Two: Management ability and integrity

Q8:	How many years has the company been in business? >15 years $= 20$; >7 years $= 10$; less $= 0$	20
Q9:	How are CEO and CFO appointed? on merit $= 20$; one or both "political" or "family" appointments $= 0$	0
Q10:	Has there been any scandal in the past two years? No $= 10$; Yes $= 0$. Has there been any "dispute" with the authorities in the last two years? No $= 10$; Yes $= 0$	10
Q11:	Was at least one executive a senior government official or minister or is one a political appointee? Yes $= 10$; No $= 0$	0
Q12:	Is there evidence of an effective strategic response to market and/or competitive forces in the last three years? Yes $= 30$; No $= 0$	30
Subsection score (actual/converted)		60 1.67

Section Three: Market risk

Q13:	Are your competitors offering or providing unsecured credit to the customer? Yes $= 50$; No $= 0$	50
Q14:	Does your company wish to increase its market share? Yes $= 20$; No $= 0$	0
Q15:	What is your potential sustainable profit margin on sales to this customer? High $= 50$; Medium $= 20$; Low $= 0$	0
Q16:	Is this customer a potential buyer of "no-value-goods" or "high-retention-cost" goods? Yes $= 40$; No $= 0$	0
Q17:	Is this customer operating in a regional market that is depressed, without having any counteracting exposure? No $= 20$; Yes $= 0$	0
Q18:	Is this customer operating in a type of trade that is depressed, without having any counteracting exposure? No $= 20$; Yes $= 0$	0
Subsection score (actual/converted)		50 4.00

Section Four: Country risk

Q19: Is this customer based in an OECD member country? Yes = 100 (and   100
other questions in this section = 0); No = 0

Q20: What is the FitchRatings' long-term foreign currency sovereign rating?   0
AAA/AA = 60; A/BBB = 50; BB = 40; B = 30; CCC = 20; CC = 10; C/
D = 0

Q21: What is the host country production of the product you are exporting,   0
as a percentage of host country consumption? <25% = 40; <50% = 30;
<75% = 20; more = 0

Subsection score (actual/converted)	100	1.00

Section Five: Selected score exaggerator

Add together the scores from QA1, Q12, Q13, Q17, Q18 and the Section Four total then enter the sum here	200	
Subsection score (actual/converted)	200	32.77

Overall trade credit risk score	*2.39*
Trade credit rating	*BBB+*
Maximum trade credit limit indication ($ millions)	*17.57*
Restricted to normal business requirement of ($ million)	*10*

V   COMPANY C

DuPont analysis Company C 1998 financials ($ millions)

Sales	12 021.53	
Costs of goods sold	10 805.84	
Other expenses (excluding interest)	982.52	
Return on sales before interest		1.94%
Net interest paid	126.95	
Return on sales after interest		0.88%
Assets		
Other current (including cash)	176.25	
Accounts receivable	265.44	
Inventory	1 077.30	
Fixed assets	3 685.29	
Asset turnover		230.99%
Liabilities		
Accounts payable	651.41	
Overdraft/notes payable	1.61	
Other current	751.68	
Long term	2 525.12	
Net tangible equity	1274.46	
Leverage		408.35%
Return on equity		18.03%
Return on equity after interest		8.33%
Defensive interval	2.53 days	

Section One A: Financial information

QA1: What is the financial analysis summary score?	20
QA2: Is the audit report clean (unqualified)? Yes = 10; No or financials Not audited = 0	10
QA3: How recent is the financial information? <6 months old = 10; <1 year old = 6; <18 months old = 2; older = 0	10
QA4: What is the customer's equity at risk? > twice the proposed limit = 20; >equal to = 10; > half = 5; less = 0	20
QA5: What is the customer's defensive interval? >32 days = 20; >16 days = 16; >8 days = 10; >4 days = 4; less = 0	0
QA6: Was cash flow from operations minus dividends positive? Yes = 20; No = 0	20
QA7: What is the "days payables outstanding" number equal to? Normal terms = 20; less than 150% of Normal = 10; more = 0	20

One A: Subsection score (actual/converted)	100	1.00

Table: Financial strength assessment

	Summary	Score
Customer's financial strength is judged to be	Marginal	20

Section Two: Management ability and integrity

Q8: How many years has the company been in business? >15 years = 20; >7 years = 10; less = 0	20
Q9: How are CEO and CFO appointed? On merit = 20; one or both "political" or "family" appointments = 0	20
Q10: Has there been any scandal in the past two years? No = 10; Yes = 0. Has there been any "dispute" with the authorities in the last two years? No = 10; Yes = 0	20
Q11: Was at least one executive a senior government official or minister or is one a political appointee? Yes = 10; No = 0	0
Q12: Is there evidence of an effective strategic response to market and/or competitive forces in the last three years? Yes = 30; No = 0	30

Subsection score (actual/converted)	90	1.11

Section Three: Market risk

Q13:	Are your competitors offering or providing unsecured credit to the customer? Yes = 50; No = 0	50	
Q14:	Does your company wish to increase its market share? Yes = 20; No = 0	0	
Q15:	What is your potential sustainable profit margin on sales to this customer? High = 50; Medium = 20; Low = 0	0	
Q16:	Is this customer a potential buyer of "no-value-goods" or "high-retention-cost" goods? Yes = 40; No = 0	0	
Q17:	Is this customer operating in a regional market that is depressed, without having any counteracting exposure? No = 20; Yes = 0	20	
Q18:	Is this customer operating in a type of trade that is depressed, without having any counteracting exposure? No = 20; Yes = 0	0	
Subsection score (actual/converted)		70	2.86

Section Four: Country risk

Q19:	Is this customer based in an OECD member country? Yes = 100 (and other questions in this section = 0); No = 0	100	
Q20:	What is the FitchRatings' long-term foreign currency sovereign rating? AAA/AA = 60; A/BBB = 50; BB = 40; B = 30; CCC = 20; CC = 10; C/D = 0	0	
Q21:	What is the host country production of the product you are exporting, as a percentage of host country consumption? <25% = 40; <50% = 30; <75% = 20; more = 0	0	
Subsection score (actual/converted)		100	1.00

Section Five: Selected score exaggerator

Add together the scores from QA1, Q12, Q13, Q17, Q18 and the Section Four total then enter the sum here	220	
Subsection score (actual/converted)	220	22.38

Overall trade credit risk score	*1.67*
Trade credit rating	*A+*
Maximum trade credit limit indication ($ millions)	*323.99*
Restricted to normal business requirement of ($ millions)	*52*

VI   COMPANY D

Financial estimates only for Company D 2000 ($ millions)

Cost of goods sold	2000.0
Net tangible equity	80.0

Section One B: Financial information

QB1: Are financial statements available? No = 0	0	
QB2: How many days late is the customer reported to pay creditors? <5 = 30; <30 = 10; more = 0	30	
QB3: Has any one of the owners or executives been involved in a failed business? No = 10; Yes = 0	10	
QB4: Is there evidence of extravagant expenditure (spending out of line with Normal expected income levels in their business) either within the business or by executives in their private capacity? No = 30; Yes = 0	0	
QB5: Does the customer have an active account with a well-respected bank that is active in the appropriate market? Yes = 5; No = 0	5	
QB6: Is customer's legal counsel a reputable firm? Yes = 5; No = 0	5	
QB7: Have any key employees resigned in the past three months ? No = 20; Yes = 0	20	
One B: Subsection score (actual/converted)	70	1.43

Section Two: Management ability and integrity

Q8: How many years has the company been in business? >15 years = 20; >7 years = 10; less = 0	10	
Q9: How are CEO and CFO appointed? On merit = 20; one or both "political" or "family" appointments = 0	20	
Q10: Has there been any scandal in the past two years? No = 10; Yes = 0. Has there been any "dispute" with the authorities in the last two years? No = 10; Yes = 0	10	
Q11: Was at least one executive a senior government official or minister or is one a political appointee? Yes = 10; No = 0	10	
Q12: Is there evidence of an effective strategic response to market and/or competitive forces in the last three years? Yes = 30; No = 0	30	
Subsection score (actual/converted)	80	1.25

Section Three: Market risk

Q13: Are your competitors offering or providing unsecured credit to the customer? Yes = 50; No = 0	50
Q14: Does your company wish to increase its market share? Yes = 20; No = 0	20
Q15: What is your potential sustainable profit margin on sales to this customer? High = 50; Medium = 20; Low = 0	0
Q16: Is this customer a potential buyer of "No-value-goods" or "high-retention-cost" goods? Yes = 40; No = 0	0
Q17: Is this customer operating in a regional market that is depressed, without having any counteracting exposure? No = 20; Yes = 0	0
Q18: Is this customer operating in a type of trade that is depressed, without having any counteracting exposure? No = 20; Yes = 0	20

Subsection score (actual/converted)	90	2.22

Section Four: Country risk

Q19: Is this customer based in an OECD member country? Yes = 100 (and other questions in this section = 0); No = 0	0
Q20: What is the FitchRatings' long-term foreign currency sovereign rating? AAA/AA = 60; A/BBB = 50; BB = 40; B = 30; CCC = 20; CC = 10; C/D = 0	40
Q21: What is the host country production of the product you are exporting, as a percentage of host country consumption? <25% = 40; <50% = 30; <75% = 20; more = 0	0

Subsection score (actual/converted)	40	2.50

Section Five: Selected score exaggerator

Add together the scores from QB2, QB4, Q12, Q13, Q17, Q18 and the Section Four total then enter the sum here	170

Subsection score (actual/converted)	170	62.77

Overall trade credit risk score	*4.13*
Trade credit rating	*B*
Maximum trade credit limit indication ($ millions)	*24.23*

Bibliography

Altman, E. I. and Narayanan, P. (1997) An International Survey of Business Failure Classification Models – *Financial Markets, Institutions and Instruments*, **6**(2), May, New York University Salomon Center.

Business Week (2002) European Edition, 6 May (ISSN 0007-7135) (http://www.businessweek europe. com).

Carayol, R. and Firth, D. (2001) *Corporate Voodoo*, Capstone Publishing Ltd, Oxford, UK.

Carter, N. (1987) Country Risk Assessment, in *International Finance and Investment*, Terry, B. (ed.), Bankers Books Ltd, London.

Effros, R. C. (1994) *Current Legal Issues Affecting Central Banks*, Vol. 2, IMF, Washington, DC.

French, P. and Gai, D. (2003) Unlocking Shareholder Value through Managed Services for Order-to-Cash, a White Paper on the Equitant corporate website (http://www.equitant. com).

Gallinger, G. W. Various publications and presentations about *cash flow analysis*, the *cash flow cycle* and the *defensive interval* available at: http://www.public.asu.edu/~bac524/.

Gallinger, G. W. (1995) *An Evaluation of Techniques for Monitoring Accounts Receivable*, National Association of Credit Management, Columbia, MD.

Hagerty, J. (2001) *CFOs Tell Banks – Electronically Support My Business or Else . . .* AMR CFO Report (http://www.amrresearch.com).

Henschel, P. (2001) Understanding and Winning the Never-Ending Search for Talent, an article that appeared in http://www.linezine.com.

International Chamber of Commerce (ICC) publications *UCP 500, eUCP Version 1.0, ISP98, URDG 458, URC 322*, ICC Publishing SA at: http://www.iccbooks.com.

Johnson, S. (1998) *Who Moved My Cheese?*, Random House Group Limited, London.

Lawton, S. (2002) Managing Director European Corporates, Moody's Investors Service Limited, International Energy Credit Association Conference presentation, June.

Mulford, C. W. and Comiskey, E. E. (2002) *The Financial Numbers Game*, John Wiley & Sons, Inc., New York.

Payne, S. (2003) The Keys to Unlocking Hidden Cash, an article for REL Consultancy Group (http://www.relconsult.com).

Scase, R. (2000) The Migration of Management to Leadership, a verbal presentation reported on web page http://www.barrettwells.co.uk/profscase.htm.

The Credit and Financial Management Review (1997), **3**(2), April–June, Credit Research Foundation (http://www.crfonline.org).

Index

Index compiled by Annette Musker